Creative
Grandparenting

Discovery House PUBLISHERS

BOX 3566 • GRAND RAPIDS, MI 49501

*PUBLISHING BOOKS THAT FEED
THE SOUL WITH THE WORD OF GOD.*

Creative
Grandparenting

How to Love and Nurture a New Generation

Jerry and Jack Schreur
with Judy and Leslie Schreur

Creative Grandparenting
How to Love and Nurture and New Generation

Copyright © 1992 by Jerry Schreur and Jack Schreur

Library of Congress Cataloging in Publication Data

Schreur, Jerry, 1941—
    Creative Grandparenting : how to love and nurture
a new generation / Jerry Schreur, Jack Schreur :
with Judy Schreur and Leslie Schreur.
        p.   cm.
    ISBN 0-929239-67-9
    1. Grandparenting. 2. Grandparent and child. 3. Children—
Religious life. I. Schreur, Jack, 1964– . II. Title.
306.874'5—dc20   92-37042
                                      CIP

Discovery House Publishers is affiliated with Radio Bible Class, Grand Rapids, Michigan.

Discovery House books are distributed to the trade by Thomas Nelson Publishers, Nashville, Tennessee 37214.

Printed in the United States of America

92 93 94 95 96 / CHG / 10 9 8 7 6 5 4 3 2 1

Dedication

Jerry: For Lauren, Erin, Elena, Jonathan, and Kendall, my wonderful grandchildren, who inspired me to write this book.

Jack: For Leslie my wife, and Erin, Jonathan, and Kendall my children, I love you. For my father, who is both my friend and teacher, thanks.

Acknowledgments

Jack and I would like to thank Carol Holquist for caring about grandparents and for believing in *Creative Grandparenting*. Her faith in us and her excitement for the subject made this book possible. We would also like to thank David Egner for his invaluable help with the manuscript. Dave's knowledge and skill gave life to our words and ideas, and we are grateful for his involvement with *Creative Grandparenting*. Finally, we would like to thank the grandparents and families who shared their lives with us. Thank you for being creative, involved grandparents and for letting us share your stories in this book.

Contents

Preface   ix
Foreword: Creative Grandparenting Is for You!   11
One: The Wonder Years   19
Two: The Middle Years   37
Three: Time With Teenagers   55
Four: When the Family Is Falling Apart   77
Five: Long-Distance Grandparenting   99
Six: You and Your Children   125
Seven: Involvement Versus Interference   147
Eight: Grandparenting With a Difference   167
Nine: Faith of Our Fathers   183
Afterword: Just Do It!   209

Preface

Creative Grandparenting really began almost eight years ago on a snowy February morning when Judy and I learned that we had a granddaughter. She weighed seven pounds, five ounces, and her parents named her Lauren Jessica. I didn't know it then, but that small package was to change my life dramatically. Being a grandfather fascinated and challenged me in a way that I hadn't imagined. With the arrival of each new grandchild, the fascination grew.

Two years ago, I sat down with my son Jack to talk about some writing projects I had in mind. At the end of the conversation I casually mentioned that more than anything I would like to write about grandparenting. Jack walked away laughing, only to come back two days later with the title *Creative Grandparenting* and some great ideas. In the last two years we have researched grandparenting, interviewed grandparents, and read just about everything written on the subject.

Although *Creative Grandparenting* is soundly researched, it is much more the product of my love of being a grandfather and the sheer joy and excitement I experience when I'm with my grandchildren. Yet as I talked with grandparents, even though most of them enjoyed their role, many seemed to need some encouragement to really get involved with grandparenting. *Creative Grandparenting* is written to inspire grandparents to do just that: To give you a sense of the difference you can make in the lives of your grandchildren, and to help you see how creative grandparenting can change your life.

Our contention is that being a creative grandparent doesn't take any special skills or abilities. It doesn't require a great deal of money or a big house or an outgoing personality. It isn't dependent on education or profession, anyone can do it. All creative grandparenting takes is love, and the desire to express that love in as many ways as possible.

Our hope is that *Creative Grandparenting* will give you a glimpse of the purpose and meaning of grandchildren can bring into your life. And our prayer is that our stories and suggestions give you the impetus to grandparent creatively, to become a positive force, especially for God, in the lives of your grandchildren.

Creative Grandparenting Is for You!

Seven-year-old Gwen bounded into the house. Grandma was on the phone with a friend. "Grandma, quick! I need to show you something."

"Shhh, just a minute Gwen. I'm on the phone." Gwen turned a couple of pirouettes, looked at Grandma, and said louder, "Grandma, please! We have to hurry."

"Gwen, I'm almost done. Be patient." Grandma Rose could not conceal a little smile. Gwen was fairly bursting. Rose quickly ended her conversation, stretched out her hand, and said, "Okay, Gwen, what's the big emergency?"

"Grandma, follow me! Quick!" Gwen ran down the hall and out the door. Rose came as fast as she could, wishing she had the energy and vitality of her eight-year-old granddaughter. She followed Gwen past the barn, down the path to the river, across the bridge, and into the woods. Gwen had stopped and was looking into a ravine at a small tree. "Look, Grandma, look! They're just being born." Rose looked into the tree and saw three eggs, two already broken open and the third with a slight crack. They watched in silence as three robins staggered noisily into the world. Gwen and Rose spontaneously reached out for each other and held hands.

Gwen looked up at her grandma and saw tears streaking her face. "What's wrong, Grandma? Are you all right?"

"Gwen, I'm fine. Better than fine. I'm feeling as good as I ever have. I was just thinking about the day you were born. You were so tiny, and yet your lungs were so powerful. How you cried whenever they took you from your mother those first two days in the hospital! You had lots of dark hair, and I was the proudest grandma in the world. I thought that you were the most beautiful child ever. I held you that first day, and I fell in love with you. Today I feel so close to you, watching those birds making their first sounds, seeing the joy and gentleness on your face. Thanks for sharing that with me. I love you."

"Grandma, I love you too. And thanks for being my friend."

Grandparenting is a special job and a remarkable privilege. As grandparents to five wonderful, energetic children, Judy and I are continually amazed at how large a role grandparenting plays in our lives. We weren't prepared for this. We never anticipated our career as grandparents.

All we associated with our children's growth into adulthood was a quiet house and more time to ourselves. We believed that after our children were grown and living on their own, we could relax and have some fun. We're definitely having fun, but we're still waiting to relax. As for the quiet house, it may not be a reality for many years to come.

Judy and I had two children, and we thought they kept us busy. Now our house is sometimes filled with the joyful sounds of five grandchildren; all of them talking at once, each trying to outdo the other. We have never been happier. Quite simply, grandparenting has become the most important part of our lives. It's bigger than our jobs, bigger than our plans for retirement, and much bigger than our dream of a relaxed life in a quiet house. We believe that being a grandparent is the best thing in the world. And after talking to hundreds of other grandparents, we've discovered that we are not alone.

Henry loves showing his grandson how to build things. An accomplished carpenter and craftsman, Henry finds joy in passing along his skill to his twelve-year-old grandson.

Joan used to wonder what she would do after the last of her five children left home. She actually thought she might be bored or lonely. Joan's seventh grandchild is due any day, and she laughs at her earlier concern. "I can't believe how fulfilled and happy being a good grandma makes me feel." As an aside she adds, "I read a book last year on the empty-nest syndrome. I couldn't identify with that problem. I had a hard time even getting the book read. My youngest granddaughter was visiting, and she was crawling all over me."

Jim and Sandra watched their grandchild spend the first three weeks of her life in the hospital. They cried when it looked like little Samantha wasn't going to make it home. Their tears turned into celebration when Samantha survived, and then began to thrive. Her brush with death has brought them closer to her and to their own children. Jim is not an emotional man, but when he speaks about Samantha today his voice breaks and his eyes cloud with tears. "I love that little girl so much," he says quietly.

Ask these grandparents what the best part of their lives is and they will give you the same answer: "Grandparenting." Ask them what they most look forward to and they will reply, "Time with my grandchildren." Spend time with them and they will regale you with tales of their beloved grandchildren. These people are creative grandparents, and they wouldn't miss being with their grandchildren for anything.

Grandparenting is a unique and special joy. We can delight in the love and affection of our grandchildren without having to parent them. We can watch them grow into young men and women without having to keep track of curfew or worry about their school work. Grandparenting offers all the best things about parenting without the accompanying weight of responsibility. We can be free to enjoy our grandchildren in a way that we may not have been able to enjoy our children. We are no longer newlyweds trying to deal with careers, mortgages, and the stresses of a young family. We are older, seasoned, perhaps grown less rigid with the passing of years. We're more ready to laugh and cry, better prepared to love without reservation.

There are biological grandparents and there are creative grandparents. Grandparents carry pictures in their wallets and hang photos on the wall. Grandparents have sporadic contact with their grandchildren and limited input into their lives. Regular grandparents are gift-givers and perfunctory hug-receivers.

Creative grandparents carry memories in their hearts and love in their souls. Creative grandparents go beyond showing off their grandchildren as trophies. Creative grandparents want to be an integral part of their grandchildren's lives. They want to impart to them their Christian values. They want to shower them with love and acceptance. They want to build a relationship that will last a lifetime. Creative grandparents put their hearts and souls into grandparenting, and they make a difference in the lives of their grandchildren.

This book is about creative grandparenting. This book is about going beyond the occasional phone call. We hope to challenge you to take grandparenting seriously. We desire to help you realize that grandparents can have a profound influence on their grandchildren. We want to inspire you to be creative grandparents.

We believe that grandchildren benefit greatly from a strong relationship with their grandparents. Studies show heightened self-esteem, greater chance of success in later life, and a stronger sense of family values in adults who have had good relationships with their grandparents. The facts are in. They tell us that, now more than ever, children need love and acceptance. Now more than ever, children need a significant adult to tell them that they are okay. Now more than ever, children need role models. Now more than ever, children need to see adults living out their Christianity with honesty and integrity.

Grandparents are in a terrific position to provide love and unconditional acceptance. They are the ideal people to foster a sense of value and self-worth in children. They can be great role models. They can be people of faith, men and women of the Word, leaders for a new generation.

As much as our grandchildren need us, we need our grandchildren. It is a symbiotic relationship. The benefits of being a creative, involved grandparent are many. Our grandchildren give us life; we provide for them experience. They lend us enthusiasm; we bestow on them our years-earned wisdom. Grandchildren give us a renewed sense of what is possible. They give birth to new hope in

us, reminding us of things we have forgotten about ourselves and teaching us things we've never known.

When interviewing grandparents we constantly
heard the phrase, "My grandchildren keep me young."
They do. They show our tired bodies what it is like to run
barefoot through the summer grass. They inspire us by
scaling the trees we climbed in our youth. Through their
youthful enthusiasm they remind us of days long past.

They also let us into the world of young people today. One grandmother we know actually listens to the
music of her teenage grandson. She says, "I just want to
know what's going on in the world, and John helps me
stay in touch. He never treats me like an 'old fogey,' but
thinks it's kind of neat to lend me his tapes. He even
brags to his friends that his grandma likes to 'rock.' In
America, people our age are expected to retire and get out
of the way. Often we are isolated from our families and
the mainstream of society. Our grandchildren bring us
back. They provide us with an entrance into the world
again, a ticket to American culture. We need them, and
they need us."

But creative grandparenting is not all hugs and kisses. We have a responsibility to communicate our values
and our faith to our grandchildren. The thesis of this
book is that grandparents can be heroes of faith to grandchildren. We serve God by teaching our grandchildren
about Jesus. We are convinced that living out our Christianity will help our grandchildren as they grow up and
decide whether or not to follow Jesus.

Creative Grandparenting is written for every person
who wants to make a difference in the lives of his or her
grandchildren. This book is for grandparents who want
to love their grandchildren with actions and not just

words. Through *Creative Grandparenting* you will meet other grandparents and hear their stories. You will share their love and their heartache. You will begin to see just how important a role we can play in the lives of our grandchildren, regardless of their age—or ours.

Most of all, we hope that *Creative Grandparenting* will inspire you to dedicate yourself to being a creative, involved grandparent. It is not the easy road. With the joy and the happiness we can also expect pain and disappointment. But, as the other grandparents you will meet in this book will testify, we guarantee that you will not regret your decision to become a creative grandparent. You will laugh as you have never laughed, cry more deeply than you thought possible, and live with more vitality than ever before because you will be that most blessed of people, a creative grandparent.

Chapter One

The Wonder Years

The sailor-adventurers who set out from Europe on voyages of discovery hundreds of years ago were entering the unknown. They were going where no one had ever been before. They were a superstitious lot, seeing the instability of wind and water as a result of the whims of capricious and resentful gods. The uncertainty of their destination and the unknown terrors that might await them inspired a deep longing for the safety of familiar waters and welcoming harbors.

Imagine a world like that. A world where all the mysteries we adults figured out long ago are still unfathomable perplexities. Imagine a world where every new noise inspires curiosity and fear; where every new form requires investigation and understanding. This is the world of your preschool grandchildren. Like sailors of old, they too are setting off on a daring voyage of discovery. They too long for the safety of familiar waters even as they take their first tottering steps toward independence.

Grandma and Grandpa can serve as guides through these years of wonder. They can help grandchildren explore and learn how to feel at home amid the beauty and excitement of their new world. They can also be harbors of refuge when that world turns hostile and the young explorers' fears become overwhelming.

Getting started

He wasn't comfortable when he first held her. She was tiny and wrinkled; his hands were big and awkward, and he felt foolish. He thought he might crush her. He held her gingerly against himself, so softly that he could scarcely feel her little heart beating against his own. He caught a scent of her breath, smelling ever so slightly of Elmer's glue. He longed to press her form into his own—to never let her go. His heart was gone! His two-day-old granddaughter had stolen it.

The first year of life is crucial for children to gain a sense of trust that will outweigh their mistrust according to child psychologist and author Erik Erikson. Studies show conclusively that caregivers who don't interact with their babies foster mistrust in them. The duty and joy of creative grandparenting is to be, along with the parents, caregivers who build trust.

Sometimes grandparents, especially grandfathers, are more frightened than the babies themselves of their new relationships and roles. That's because babies do the unexpected when Grandma and Grandpa baby-sit them. For instance, I never got used to holding my granddaughters or grandsons when their eyes squeezed shut, their faces turned red, and their diapered bottoms rumbled in my hands and turned warm. I knew what was ahead—and behind. As any grandfather would, I ignored it as long as possible. Until the state-of-the-art, high-tech, space-age disposable diaper would begin to leak.

But creative grandparents don't ignore rumbling bottoms. They take this opportunity to express their love and build trust with their grandchildren. All the while they carry on a one-sided conversation. "Erin, you have a poopy diaper. Yes, you do. Oh yes, you do. Come here, let's get that diaper off. Oh, you are so beautiful, so special. Grandpa loves you. Yes, he does. Yes, he does."

Not the most literate of conversations. But it is important. Constantly reassuring your grandchildren strengthens their trust in you—and in themselves. Diaper changing and baby talk may appear to be beneath your dignity, but creative grandparents must seize every opportunity to express their love.

Grandparenting during infancy

Understanding three simple keys to grandparenting infants will make this time a rewarding and joyful experience. The first key is to **be available**. New parents need help. It has been said often and truthfully that babies don't come with instructions. Especially if this grandchild is a first child, your children are going to be proud, excited, independent, scared, worried, and lonely all at the same time. Parents need grandparents who are available to help with the multitude of chores during the baby's first year. Seemingly mundane tasks such as laundry, cooking, getting to the bank, and shopping can be difficult to accomplish as parents juggle schedules, work, and a young child. Grandparents who are committed to creatively become a part of their grandchildren's lives will make themselves available to meet all kinds of needs.

The second key to grandparenting during infancy is to **stay in the background**. How many times we have seen grandparents who desire to "help the new mother out" but instead become bossy and domineering. "Here, put a sweater on that baby," "You're not going to pick him up just because he's crying are you?" "When you were a baby we wouldn't have dressed you like that," "You don't want my advice? Well, remember, I've had a little more experience than you!" Grandparents who want to be available also need to stay out of the way, in the background.

The third key to grandparenting babies is simple yet probably the most important of all: **Enjoy the wonder.** Take time to be with your new grandchild; just hold her and thrill to the love and joy this little life brings. Take time to enjoy the wonder of babies.

Grandparenting during infancy is exciting. We get to share in the special joy of new life first becoming aware of the world. We do this by being available. Helping our children by baby-sitting and doing the little things. We grandparent creatively by staying in the background. No unsolicited advice, no guilt or manipulation; just affirmation and quiet love. We grandparent infants by celebrating their wonder. There is absolutely nothing so awesome as new life coming into the world. Shake yourself free from your duties, release your mind from your concerns and worries, and revel in the joy and unexpected pleasures of babies.

The preschool years

The years that follow infancy will be filled with excitement. These little bundles soon turn into dynamos of constant motion. Not a glance do they toss behind to see what they might have missed as they rush to learn and grow. These tiny persons awaken in their grandparents a profound sense of astonishment. They fill our lives with surprise.

These preschool years are wonder years—both for the children and their grandparents. Both are discovering the world. The children are seeing it for the first time. Their grandparents are seeing it anew, as if for the first time, through the eyes of their grandchildren.

Creative grandparenting during these wonder years is a joyful, life-affirming experience. Perhaps at no other time are grandchildren so open to their grandparents, so eager to trust, so willing to be kissed, hugged, and loved. About these years child psychologist David Elkind wrote:

> Preschool children seem to show a particular affinity for grandparents. Perhaps they sense a maturity and stability that is only partial in parents who are still trying to sort out parenting, marriage, and career roles. Because young children are experiencing so much that is new, it is reassuring and comforting to them to have adults who are at ease with themselves and their world. With such adults they can feel free to explore their environment. They can try out new words and activities with a sense that the world is secure and that their explorations will be understood as just that—explorations, not mischief. — David Elkind, *Grandparenting*

Grandparents walk a fine line with these intrepid little adventurers. In full support and cooperation with the parents, Grandma and Grandpa can help them venture out and explore the sometimes harsh ways of the world. We can also be lighthouses, calling our venturesome grandchildren back to safety. We have to let them learn, sometimes through painful failure, and keep them from becoming discouraged. We encourage them to overcome their fears, while we understand that fears are reasonable for a tiny child in a vast, mysterious world.

Communicating love

As children grow, their ability to communicate grows with them. Each phase gives their grandparents fresh op-

portunities to express their love. It also challenges them
to acquire the skills of a linguist as they try to compre-
hend their grandchildren's undeveloped verbal expres-
sions. One-sided conversations gradually become punctuated with an occasional, treasured "gub oo bampa."

Talks with grandchildren can be a nearly continuous
stream of love. This does not mean that we need to say
"I love you" 300 times a day. Rather, the language should
be open and inviting, the tone reassuring, the manner
loving. Grandchildren should be able to feel the fire of
love that burns in their grandparents' hearts. It should be
apparent while Grandma is rocking one to sleep, or while
Grandpa is cleaning out the garage with his two-year-old
granddaughter's capable assistance.

Love-communication is not limited to speech. Non-
verbal signals are equally important. One study revealed
that about 7 percent of the message is delivered by the actual words. Tone of voice conveys 38 percent and nonver-
bal signals account for 55 percent of what we communicate. Even with very young grandchildren, what we
say pales in importance when compared with what we
do.

Creative grandparents know the value of a hug. One
grandfather we know is appreciated for his hugs. They
are generous and abundant: very tight and very long.
And his grandchildren love them! He wants them to get
the idea that he will love them forever. And while he
holds his preschool grandchildren tightly, he gives them
a steady stream of verbal affirmation. With words and actions, he is speaking volumes.

How do grandparents make the most of these precious years? How does Grandma or Grandpa give those
little explorer-adventurers what they need most from

them? We'd like to offer eight hints for creative grandparents of two- to five-year-olds.

Creative grandparenting hint #1:
Love your grandchildren all ways

Grandparents cannot express their love too much, too often, or in too many ways to their wonder-years grandchildren. We are not spoiling them when we give them constant reassurances of our love. On the contrary, we will find it easier to say no to them because they already know that we love them.

Creative grandparents make an unflagging commitment to finding new ways to say "I love you." We accept this biblical principle as our mandate: "My little children, let us not love in word or in tongue, but in deed and in truth" (1 John 3:18).

One way we can do it is by mail. When grandparents are on a vacation, take the time to send a postcard to each of your grandchildren. Make sure to mail them separately. Preschool children seldom receive personal mail, and they are thrilled when Mom or Dad reads a card sent personally to them.

After a trip to the Grand Canyon, my wife Judy and I were greeted with these words from our granddaughter: "You wrote a letter just to me. I saved it and put it up on my wall." Her father reported that the arrival of that letter was the highlight of her week—and it took us only five minutes to write and mail it.

Another way creative grandparents show their love is by reading to their grandchildren. In a world of, "Hurry up! Get your coat on! I told you to go potty five minutes ago. Weren't you listening? Come on, we're late," grandparents can slow down to be with their grandchildren.

We have the time to read them their favorite story—
again, and again, and again.

We can also converse with them and listen to them.
Children have a profound need to be spoken to and
heard. We build trust and self-acceptance in our grandchildren simply by listening as they chatter on about
anything and everything that pops into their active little
brains.

Here's how it goes: "Grandpa, who makes squirrels?
What do you mean, they're born? I know that. But who
makes them? You say God made them? Why? Does God
love squirrels? Does He love me like He loves squirrels?
More? I'm glad you love me too, Grandpa."

Creative grandparenting hint #2:
Look and listen

Pay close attention to your wonder-years grandchildren.
Observe them carefully. Listen to what they say. Learn
their habits and idiosyncrasies. Then show them that
you value them by acting on your understanding of the
little things that make them tick.

Grandpa Jim is on the board of his church. People
need to see him. But he aggravates some of the big people
at church. Why? Because when they are looking all over
for him after the service, he is not available. They invariably find him in his grandson's Sunday school classroom
(with Mom's and Dad's permission). He will be sprawled
on the floor, eye-to-eye with little Christopher, listening
to an account of a trip to the supermarket with his mom.
This is his grandson's time, and he doesn't let anyone rob
him of it. He feels that he is applying these words of
Christ: "Let the little children come to Me and do not for-
bid them; for of such is the kingdom of heaven" (Matt.

19:14). Jim feels that if Jesus esteemed the little ones, so should he.

Creative grandparents build time into their schedules to listen to their grandchildren. One grandmother likes to take hers "out for lunch," often to a place of the child's choosing. Okay, it's usually McDonald's. But the child who is given the opportunity to choose is being sent an important message about her worth, her value as a person. Besides, these lunch dates open up wonderful opportunities for conversation, and the most amazing things may surface.

"Going for a ride in Grandpa's blue truck" has become a great adventure for another set of grandchildren. It may only be a Saturday morning trip to the hardware store, but a stop at the donut shop gives Grandpa time to listen. He has found that his wonder-years grandson and granddaughter both enjoy these jaunts.

When you listen to your granddaughter talk about her friend Jennifer or her latest adventure at preschool, you communicate volumes to her. You tell her that she is important and that her experiences and feelings are significant. As you treat her opinions and interests with value, you are telling her that she has great value.

The wonder years are vital in a child's acceptance of his or her sexual identity. Grandparents can help with this very important aspect of development. When a grandmother applauds her "little man's" athletic exploits, or admires how much he looks like Daddy or Grandpa in his jeans and flannel shirt, she helps him see and accept himself as male. And Grandpa helps his granddaughter frame and appreciate her feminine identity when he says, "My granddaughter Kelsey's the prettiest girl in the whole church." Or, "My, you are just beautiful in that dress."

Looking. Listening. Conversing. Sure, it's an effort to find the time and to get down to their eye-level. But it pays rich, rich dividends for them—and for you.

Creative grandparenting hint #3:
Encourage and answer questions

Wonder-years grandchildren are always pondering the complexities of life. They have difficult questions that need satisfying answers. Mom and Dad can't answer them all. Grandparents can help.

Just as God listens intently when we ask, seek, and knock through prayer (Matt. 7:7), so we need to focus our attention on the asking, seeking, and knocking of our grandchildren. And just as God gives, helps us find, and opens in answer to our prayers, so we need to answer our grandchildren's many questions.

Children deserve truthful answers. Their natural, insatiable curiosity is the engine that powers their learning. True, we may get tired of the incessant questions of a two- or three-year-old. We may become frustrated trying to explain the innumerable complexities of our world to an inquisitive four-year-old. But they have a need to know and a right to know. Besides, if we keep answering, they'll keep asking—right on through the important teenage years.

Five-year-old Erin was unusually quiet, deep in thought. After a few minutes she seriously asked a question that was weighing heavily on her mind. That question deserved an answer of equal seriousness, even though it was unimportant on an adult level, and Grandma gave it to her. Asking questions is one of the important ways children learn. If we brush them off or treat their questions flippantly, we give them the message that they are not important.

How frustrating it can be when they are in the "why" stage! It goes something like this:

"Grandpa, why are there trees?"

"Because God loves beautiful things. He made the trees to make the world beautiful."

"Grandpa, why does God love beautiful things?"

"Because beautiful things make His children happy, and He wants us happy."

"Grandpa, why does God want us happy?"

"Because He loves us."

"Grandpa, why . . . ."

This kind of conversation appears to be pointless, especially if it's repeated every time you get together. But it's of great value to that child. She wants to learn about her world, and she has chosen you to show her the way. Grandparents may grow weary with all the questions, but we will gain a second wind if we remember what a privilege it is to be selected by our young explorer as a navigator through this troubled world.

The next time you spend a few hours with your wonder-years grandchild, try asking questions that require more than a yes or no answer. You may get a lot of "what" and "why" answers in return and end up exhausted after explaining everything from waves and wind to jet airplanes, but you'll have opened wonderful doors of discovery for your grandchild. And you'll have the opportunity to share your wisdom, experience, values, and faith with your exploring, questioning, learning little loved one.

Creative grandparenting hint #4:
Take risks

Paul, a successful businessman, was afraid of crying children. He found himself growing tense whenever he was around children who cried. He could control his business world with comparative ease, but he could not control a little weeper. He just did not know how to quiet them. As a result, Paul was afraid to be left alone with his infant grandchildren. Besides, his granddaughters were very attached to their mothers, which is a good thing. But for Grandpa baby-sitter, it was *not* a good thing.

So how did he find himself with this tiny screaming bundle—with no woman around to help? Simple. He asked for it. This brave executive decided to be an involved, creative grandparent, and crying babies came with the territory.

He tried reading to her: still crying. He sang to her: cried louder. Played patty-cake: looked at him like he was crazy and resumed screaming. Nothing worked. It was crisis time. Finally he set all fear aside and picked her up. He held her gently to his shoulder and talked to her quietly. The roar became a sob, and then a sniffle. Then came the gentle, rhythmic breathing of sleep. He had done it! Few things in his life could have given him so much pride and satisfaction.

Fear is the enemy of grandparenting. Fear tells Grandpa that if he climbs that tree with his active grandkids, one or all of them may fall out and break an arm. Fear tells him to worry about what others may think if he gets down on the floor and plays rambunctiously. Paul chose to overcome his fears, and he felt as much sense of accomplishment in getting his granddaughter to sleep as he would have had in closing a $6 million deal. Yet he would have never experienced that joy if he had played it safe and refused the opportunity to conquer his fear of crying babies.

The doorway to loving every moment with our grandchildren is blocked by our apprehensions. Many of our fears are irrational or based on pride. Creative grandparents learn to step over those fears and build an intimate relationship with our wonder-years grandchildren.

Creative grandparenting hint #5:
Say yes more often than no

It's all too easy to form the habit of saying no when you are asked to grandparent.

"Dad, will you watch the children this weekend so Jodi and I can get away?"

"No, Ken, I'm too busy."

"Grandpa, could you swing me?"

"We were just outside. Find something else to do."

"Grandma, will you color with me?"

"Not right now, honey. Grandma's watching television."

Saying yes more often than no means seizing every reasonable opportunity to be with your grandchildren. They only move through the wonder years once. This special time in their lives is flying past, and creative grandparents must make use of every opportunity to be with them.

Certainly there are times when it is appropriate to say no. But this should never be simply because it would inconvenience you to say yes. Grandchildren are not an inconvenience; they're a treasure. Time with them is not wasted; it is invested.

When the opportunity rises to say yes, take it. Look for ways to give positive responses to your grandchildren. They need it, and you need to see their eyes light up.

Creative grandparenting hint #6:
Be your child's playmate
When you play with your grandchildren, you will open the windows to their souls. A game of hide-and-seek reveals their fears and sense of fun. A game of chase shows their excitement. A session of drawing and painting will unleash their creativity. Playing dollies will show you their needs and values. A game of ball or plastic-pin bowling will show you their motor skills. And all of it reveals their language, thought, and moral development.

Play can also open wounds on your body. As I write, my ribs still hurt. They are a painful reminder of summer play with my grandchildren. The whole family was together. Add to that a Slip-and-Slide, and disaster was the result.

A Slip-and-Slide is a strip of plastic with a sprinkler system built in to wet down the surface. The object is to run, launch yourself into the air, and skid on your stomach the length of the plastic. Unbelievable fun!

They were outside; I was in. Soon, chants of "Grandpa! Grandpa!" echoed through the house. I reluctantly donned my bathing suit. Then I charged out of the house, achieved full speed, and dove onto the plastic. I slid the full length, continued onto the lawn, and stopped six inches from the sidewalk. Grass and mud were in my eyes, my bathing suit, my hair. The discomfort was not eased by the children's shrieks of laughter. I still hold the family record for the longest slide!

Being your grandchildren's playmate doesn't necessarily require a ride on the Slip-and-Slide. It *does* mean setting aside the newspaper, putting aside the book (even this one), and doing what they want to do. Balancing the checkbook can wait when the children are begging to play.

Playing with your grandchildren shows them that you love them and appreciate who they are. Creative grandparents treasure these moments because it gives us a peek into our grandchild's world. More importantly, playmates are friends—and that's what you want to be to your grandchild.

Jim is a retired construction worker. He has become good at Old Maid. Why? Because that's the only game his granddaughter knows how to play. So he gets lots of practice. Jim is a moose of a man, tall and weathered by the elements. The cards, which look like miniatures in his large hands, look enormous in his granddaughter's. As they play, his eyes belie his years. They dance with delight whenever she picks the Old Maid and tries not to show it.

Jim has many opportunities to be his granddaughter's playmate. They could do all kinds of things. Old Maid is their special kind of play. The only limit is the imagination and energy of grandparents, and their desire to see their wonder-years grandchildren light up the house with laughter.

Play is always a learning process, but not in a rigid, academic sense. Wonder-years children learn how the world works through play:

- It fuels their imagination and creativity.
- It helps them learn the rules of social interaction.
- It gives them a legitimate outlet for their natural exuberance.
- It gives introverted children a safe opportunity to reach out to others around them.
- It gives wonder-years children a way to express themselves.

Say yes to play!

Creative grandparenting hint #7:
Follow the child's agenda

Have you ever seen a grandmother being pulled around by her four-year-old grandson and wondered who was in charge? Don't wonder too much. That grandma is probably a creative grandparent who knows that doing what she wants is important, but doing what he wants is imperative.

Be willing to do what your grandchildren want to do and talk about what they want to talk about. Sure, it's frustrating to read that five-year-old the same story over and over again. But after that fifteenth reading, when she begins to read it back to you, you understand the reason for her request.

Because you realize that your agenda may have nothing to do with theirs, ask them what they want to do. Even if it doesn't excite you, you need to do it every once in a while. Let them pick the restaurant. Let them choose the game. Let them order their choice from the menu.

Our family participates in an activity our family calls *bummin'*. We define it as *creatively doing nothing somewhere else*. It's an activity widely practiced by grandparents who think creatively. The beauty of it is that the grandchild gets to set the agenda.

One day the agenda was garage sales. Lauren took $1.50 from her piggy bank, and we embarked on a quest to find a suitable treasure. (I was along merely to drive the car.) Several hours later, after traversing nearly every square mile of our city, we found an appropriate item: a shell necklace of dubious origin and even more questionable aesthetic value. Lauren purchased it for the bargain price of seventy-five cents and proudly presented it to

Grandma as a gift that evening. Grandma was delighted to be remembered.

Creative grandparenting means squeezing our agenda into our grandchildren's lives—not theirs into ours. At stake is their sense of importance and self-worth.

Creative grandparenting hint #8:
Love Jesus with your grandchildren

"Dear Jesus, thank You for this terrific day. Thank You for giving us life. Thank You for loving us. And Jesus, thank You for Erin. Please watch over her and protect her. I love her very much too. Amen."

"Grandma, why did you ask Jesus to take care of me?'

"Because I love you very much, and I don't want anything bad to happen to you."

"But why did you ask Jesus? Does He care about me too?"

"Yes, Erin. Jesus loves you very much. The Bible says that Jesus loves you so much that He died for you. That's a lot of love!"

"Does Jesus know my name?"

"I'm sure He does, Erin. He knows mine too. And He loves you as much as I do."

Children develop their first perceptions of God during the wonder years. They try to picture Him in their minds. They become aware that their parents and grandparents read the Bible, pray, go to church and try to follow Jesus. Creative grandparents know the importance of modeling a real and personal relationship with Christ.

Living in obedience to God and His Word, with Christ a part of everyday conversation, makes a powerful statement about the reality of your faith to your grandchildren. They know what Grandma and Grandpa believe because they watch you so closely. You cannot fake it very long in front of them. Do you see what this does? It gives you the responsibility of forging a real-live faith of your own, lived out with all its complexities and ambiguities, for their questioning, impressionable minds to see.

The Bible testifies to the power of this kind of faith in a grandparent. When the apostle Paul charged Timothy with the task of carrying out the work of the gospel, he wrote, "When I call to remembrance the genuine faith that is in you, which dwelt first in your grandmother Lois and your mother Eunice, and I am persuaded is in you also . . ." (2 Tim. 1:5).

Love Jesus with your grandchildren. There is no greater way to care for them!

Creative Grandparenting for the wonder years is:

1. Loving your grandchildren all ways.
2. Looking and listening.
3. Encouraging questions.
4. Not being afraid.
5. Saying yes more often than no.
6. Being a playmate.
7. Following their agenda.
8. Loving Jesus with them.

Creative grandparents are always making up their own rules, continually finding new ways to show love to their wonder-years grandchildren. As you live creatively with your grandchildren, you will have stories of your own. Stories of delightful, meaningful, wonder-filled moments because you chose to be a creative, involved grandparent.

Chapter Two

The Middle Years

Jeffrey walked hesitantly into the room, his head down. Grandpa looked up from his paper and saw that his eight-year-old grandson was looking sad. "What's wrong Jeff? Are you okay?"

"Grandpa, it's kind of hard to talk about. Nobody pays attention to me anymore."

"What do you mean? Of course they do. Your parents love you."

"I know they love me, but it just seems like everybody else in my family is more important than I am. John is starting high school, and Mom and Dad are always talking about him. Janie is three, and everybody always says how cute she is. Nobody ever talks about me anymore. All they do is yell at me to get out of the way or to go clean my room."

Grandpa pondered this a moment. Then he said, "Jeffrey, come here a minute. I want you to know something. Your grandma and I love you very much. We think that you're great, and we're glad you're our grandson. How would you like to spend a week with me on the sailboat this summer? Just you and me. I've already talked to your mom and dad about it, and they said it would be okay if you want to do it. I'll teach you how to navigate. We might even cross Lake Michigan to Wisconsin."

"Oh, Grandpa, could we really do that? I'd love to!"

"It's settled then. Let's go tell your mom. . . ."

The years of middle childhood, from ages six to eleven, are sometimes forgotten years. Teenagers get all the press and toddlers get all the attention. Children in the middle feel left out or in the way. It's even easy for us as grandparents to overlook them in favor of the new baby or the graduating adolescent. But that would be a terrible mistake! Children need as much if not more attention during the middle years as in any other time in their lives.

In this chapter we will look at what drives our middle-years grandchildren—what makes them tick. What are the developmental tasks of ages six to eleven? What do children this age need most from a creative grandparent? We will also identify the pitfalls of the in-between years and see how we as creative grandparents can help our grandchildren avoid them. And we will examine closely the roles we can play to best support our middle-years grandchildren.

Child development in the middle years

Get ready! Be prepared! Your grandchildren often will make a mess of things during their middle years. They will take things apart and not be able to put them back together. They will get things out and not put them away. The curiosity of the wonder-years child grows even sharper during middle childhood. Their "whys" become never-ending and their curiosity is boundless.

We will understand the reasons for these characteristics once we identify the developmental tasks of early childhood. We may define a developmental task as the major task each child needs to accomplish during a certain age span to grow up healthy and to function well in society. Achieving this task enables him or her to move successfully into the next developmental stage. In one sense, the developmental task becomes the job of the child during a particular period in his life. The job or task of middle-childhood is to develop a sense of self-sufficiency and competence. Child psychologist Erik Erikson classified this stage as *industry versus inferiority.*

During the years of middle childhood our grandchildren begin to build a sense of accomplishment. They find out whether or not they are able to compete successfully with other children. Once they reach these elementary school years, children are not protected as much by their parents. They are finding out whether they will be able to make it in the big, wide world. In using the phrase *industry versus inferiority*, Erikson meant that children of this age need to find out what they can do—what they are good at. This helps build a sense of competence. If, in the process of trying to build competence, they are continually ridiculed and put down, they will develop strong feelings of inferiority. These rambunctious, energetic kids are extremely fragile.

Cindy was crying as she ran into the house. Her breath came in short gulps and tears cascaded down her face. Her nose was running. She looked pitiful. "Cindy, what's wrong?" Mom asked. "Why are you crying? Are you hurt?"

"Oh Mom, the kids are so mean to me at school. The boys all call me names and I don't have any friends."

"What do you mean, you don't have any friends? Tell me what happened."

"I was trying to play basketball during gym class. I'm a terrible basketball player. No matter how hard I try, I can't catch the ball or shoot it in the basket. They picked teams and I was the last one picked. I knew nobody would want me on their team. Then while I was playing, I prayed and prayed that nobody would pass the ball to me. But they did, and I dropped it and kicked it out of bounds. We lost the game. Everybody laughed at me. Mom, I feel so bad. Why can't I be good at something? Everything I do turns out wrong."

"Cindy, you are only ten years old. You have a lot of time before you have to figure out what you are good at. Besides, your dad and I believe that you are the most incredible girl in the world."

Cindy is struggling with issues of competence versus inferiority. In her world, playing basketball is an important skill and she just can't measure up. That failure is producing a strong sense of inferiority in her. Cindy is beginning to believe that not only is she not a good basketball player, but that she really is not good at anything. Universalizing is common with middle-years children. Because they fail in one area, they immediately apply that failure to their entire lives.

An important aspect of building a sense of competence and self-sufficiency is learning to get along with peers and compete appropriately with them. During their preschool years, most children have been shielded from intense competition. Mom and Dad have helped their children learn to share with other children, face competition, and handle failure. When the child is in school all day, however, the parent is not there. She has to do it on her own. And this can be traumatic.

Perhaps, for example, other kids can swing all by themselves, but little Jeremy has always had Mom push him. When the bell rings for recess and the children head for the swings, Jeremy is in trouble. He can't compete.

Other children are performing at a higher lever than he is. This erodes his self-esteem. If Jeremy is doing well in his schoolwork, however, that can help offset his inability to swing with the other children.

During the middle years, children begin to compare themselves with others their age. In early childhood Mom and Dad did all the comparing, wondering if Johnny were tall enough, smart enough, or developing fast enough. Parents (and grandparents) were competing with other parents (and grandparents). In middle childhood, however, the children see for themselves how they stack up against other children. They need to be able to point to something in their lives that they can do as well as their peers, whether it's athletics or musical or scholastic achievement.

Jack was never a great athlete. In elementary school the big game was kickball, and he was terrible at it. Oh, he kicked the ball all right, but he couldn't catch it. He was afraid it would hit him in the face, so he closed his eyes before he caught the ball. His friends always picked him last for kickball teams. They laughed at him, and it hurt. .

Jack compensated for his inability to measure up in kickball by becoming very good at dodgeball. His natural quickness and fear of the ball served him well in a game where the object is to avoid getting hit. Though Jack blushed at his failures in kickball, he could take pride in his success in dodgeball. This illustrates the importance middle-years children attach to successful competition. And grandparents would be wise not to underestimate the importance of building a sense of competence in their grandchildren.

We have been talking mainly about physical skills, but this principle applies equally to intellectual and social skills. Middle-years children are always trying to determine who is the smartest student, the best athlete, the prettiest girl, or the most popular boy. Therefore, it's helpful for children who are not good athletes to do well in their schoolwork or in some other area. It's okay to have lots of friends but not be a great speller.

Some children, however, feel that they are not good at anything. They have *no* sense of accomplishment in their lives. When they look at themselves, they see failure. Instead of achieving industry, they fall into inferiority. And that's where creative grandparents can really help.

Value formation

One of the most important facets of the search for self-sufficiency is *the formulation of values and development of a system of morality.* Children are not only trying to figure out where they fit on this planet, but also how they should act. Deciding what is right and wrong, and learning how to determine good from bad, play a large part in their thinking. Because middle-years children often can't articulate their feelings well, we can easily miss this important aspect of their development. Teenagers can be much more articulate in expressing their feelings, so we are more aware of their growing faith and moral conviction. In middle childhood this is often a hidden process, but it is very important.

People who counsel troubled teenagers know that many of them did not develop a system of morality in middle childhood. About these children, parents say, "He was such a quiet child, so accepting of everything we said. Now look at him! He has turned his back on God and gone his own way." More likely, the truth is that the child never did accept his parents' values. He was just going along because it was easy. His value system was never challenged or completed. Therefore, we must not take for granted that this important task of middle childhood was achieved.

A corollary to moral development in our grandchildren is their understanding of limits and rules. Children in this stage of life are learning to live with self-imposed rules and limits. We call this *personal morality*. They are also learning to live within societal boundaries and family rules and limits. This is not always a painless or uncomplicated process. The natural ego and self-centeredness of children isn't easily tempered by rules. Coming to terms with limitations on behavior can be a long, difficult process, but it is a vital part of development. Learning to act and react within societal and family boundaries is necessary to function successfully as an adolescent, and later on as an adult.

The third aspect of the task of middle childhood is the *refinement of self-concept*. As children succeed or fail in their attempt to build competence and a system of morality, they modify their self-image accordingly. This will have a profound effect on them during adolescence. Children who enter the teenage years with a shaky self-image are not likely to exit with confidence or security. Unless preteens complete these developmental tasks, they will face a difficult transition into adulthood.

So, what does all this mean? What difference does this developmental task stuff make to creative grandparents? First, it is important to us as we try to understand our grandchildren. We need to know what they are going through and what should happen next in their development. We need to empathize with them and support them as they struggle to complete each developmental task.

Second, when we understand what is happening during the middle-childhood years, we are better able to develop a plan to help our grandchildren make it through these years with a healthy sense of self-esteem and a solid system of morality and priorities.

As we formulate this plan, we need to be aware of the areas where our grandchildren need and welcome our help. Grandparents can help their grandchildren build a sense of competence. To do that we must become their *coaches*. We can help build a healthy sense of self-esteem. We do that by becoming their *cheerleaders*. Children need encouragement as they formulate their ideas of right and wrong, good and bad. To help our grandchildren learn to accept limits and rules, we sometimes need to become *umpires*. We'll look at each of these roles more carefully.

Grandparents as coaches

How do grandparents help their middle-years grandchildren become competent and develop a sense of self-sufficiency? As creative grandparents we spark our grandchildren's innate abilities by joining their team and becoming their coaches. Most of us can point to significant adults who took us under their wings and passed along a skill to us when we were young. They gave us confidence by building our competence. Thus, as coach to our middle-childhood grandchildren, we need to boost their confidence by building their competence. We need to show them how to do something.

Joseph is a fifty-five-year-old grandfather of two. Grandpa Joe is taking seven-year-old Christopher camping this year for the first time. Joe is a skilled hiker, hunter, and camper. He spends his leisure time outdoors, in tents and on the trail. This summer Christopher will begin learning how to be a competent camper. Joe plans to teach him how to set up a tent, pack and backpack, cook over an open fire, and other skills necessary to survive in the wilderness. Chris is a shy child with few close friends. Imagine the boost to his self-esteem that will accompany his newfound competence as a camping buddy of Grandpa! Grandpa Joe is a creative grandparent who understands his grandson's need for a coach.

As coaches, we help our grandchildren build competence and become self-sufficient in two ways. The first and most obvious is by our instruction. Coaches pass along skills to their young apprentices.

When Jack and Jon were in elementary school, they spent a portion of almost every summer with their grandfather. He was a celery farmer, and every year he taught his grandsons a new skill. Jack will never forget the summer he was first allowed to pack celery on the assembly line. He thought it was the greatest thing in the world. Standing there with his gloves on amid the teenagers and adults employed by his grandfather, he felt competent and grown-up. He felt as though he was doing something worthwhile and useful. My father was acting as a coach, instructing my sons in the ways of farming. Although neither boy had a desire to spend his life as a farmer, both gained a great deal of confidence from their summers with Grandpa.

Coaches are instructors, but they are not cruel taskmasters. Middle-childhood grandchildren do not need to be pushed into anything. They don't need to be used so Grandpa and Grandma can relive past glories. They should not be ridiculed when they fail, or punished if they lose interest. The image of the good coach should conjure up the idea of gentle and patient love. As coaches, we are more interested in the process than the outcome—more concerned about the game than the score. Our goal is not to produce world-champion farmers or campers or swimmers or whatever. Our goal is to produce grandchildren with a quiet, growing confidence in themselves that is bred by competence and nourished through small successes.

The second way we coach our grandchildren is by allowing them to fail. Our success-oriented culture leaves little room for failure. Yet we know that failing almost always precedes growth and improvement. Our grandchildren may not have anyone else in their lives who lets them fail and then encourages them to get back up and try again. A good coach doesn't expect his player to get it right the first time or the second, or maybe even the tenth. Coaches allow for slow growth, characterized by three steps forward, two steps back. After a granddaughter fails, she may be down on herself, frustrated by her inability to learn the skill, or discouraged by her inability to complete the task. As gentle coaches, we can pick her up, dust her off, and send her back into it again.

Look for opportunities to coach your middle-years grandchild. Every grandparent has skills and abilities to pass on. If you feel you don't, consider learning something new along with your grandchildren. They need the sense of competence and confidence that our coaching can provide. Don't wait around for the perfect opportunity. It won't come. Pick up the phone and call your grandchildren. Invite them over, and get to work.

Grandparents as cheerleaders

As our grandchildren grow up, plenty of people will be ready and willing to tell them what is wrong with them. Your middle-years grandchild will already has a good sense of what he or she is not good at. Years of being put down by friends and family are not easily forgotten. Chances are, however, there aren't enough people who tell your granddaughter how great she is, or who tell your grandson how wonderful he is. As creative grandparents, it is our blessed privilege to be cheerleaders for our grandchildren.

Not only is a sense of competence important for middle-years children, but they also need assurance that the things they do are accepted by significant people in their lives. As creative grandparents, we certainly are among the significant people, and we can be the ones with the loudest voice cheering them on.

Some time ago we read about this kind of grandmother. She was cheering on her eleven-year-old grandson. It was gym day at school, and everybody was running and jumping and racing. Her grandson was running the 100-yard-dash, and she was on the sidelines, her gray hair blowing in the wind. She was shouting his name over and over again. "Go Mark, you can do it. Go! Go! Go! I know you can make it, Mark." She was urging her grandson on at the top of her lungs.

Her grandson had only one leg. The other was a prosthesis. He was running dead last. The other runners had already finished. But she loved her grandson, and she knew he would benefit from completing the race. After he crossed the finish line, he went over to his grandma and hugged her. He didn't let go for almost five minutes. "I did it, Grandma. Thank-you Grandma. . . ."

Each of us needs his own private cheerleader, but especially the middle-years child. So, look for something your grandchildren are doing well and praise them for it. Pay attention to them as they begin to develop abilities, and then give them sincere affirmation. Let people know that you think your grandchildren are the greatest in the world, and let them know it too.

Perhaps you've seen the television commercial for a long-distance telephone company. They ask a number of people who they call the most each month, and these people answer variously, "My mother," "My dad," "My best friend in Colorado." Then they ask a grandmother who she is going to call the most this month, and she proudly answers, "My seven-year-old grandson. He's a genius." Hurray! On nationwide television this grandma is leading the cheers for her middle-years grandchild.

Children who pass through the middle years without building an adequate self-image enter adolescence at a severe disadvantage. Some of them won't make it through their teenage years. They'll give up. Or they'll drop out of society. They may make bad decisions in high school regarding sexuality, drugs, and alcohol. It is imperative that children enter the stormy years of adolescence with someone in their corner rooting for them, cheering them on, building their self-esteem.

It isn't hard to be cheerleaders. All it takes is a little time and a lot of enthusiasm. Remember, our grandchildren have a good idea about what is wrong with them. But they may not have anyone dedicated to telling them what is right about them. Accept the assignment! Be a cheerleader for your grandchildren. Not only will you help them accomplish the developmental tasks of their middle-childhood years, you will boost them into adolescence and adulthood with healthy self-esteem.

Grandparents as umpires

One of the most important tasks of middle-childhood is the formation of a value system. Children from six to eleven spend this time of their lives trying to put together a system of morality. They are learning to act and react within societal and parental limits. To help our grandchildren accomplish this task, we need to become umpires.

When some people go to baseball games, they watch the sluggers and try to guess who is going to hit one out of the park. Other people are looking for a great fielding play. They love to watch double-plays turned with style and efficiency. Still others like to watch the coaches and the managers flash signs to their players. Not me. I like to watch the umpires. I think they have the toughest job in baseball. They have to enforce the rules of the game. They have to make split-second decisions about what is a ball and what is a strike, who is safe and who is out. They do this with thousands of screaming fans hurling abuse at them, and knowing that players and managers will second-guess them. Yet the best umpires never lose control. They calmly make the call and let the chips fall where they may. Highly-paid and higher strung athletes may argue and complain, but to no avail. The umpire has made his decision.

In many ways our role as umpire in the lives of our middle-years grandchildren is similar to baseball umps. We help them play within the rules and understand the limits. Just as baseball umps have to deal with pleading athletes, we have to deal with children who don't always see the wisdom behind the guidelines. Our job is to help our grandchildren establish a system of morality and live within it.

The question, of course, is how? How do we help our grandchildren work out their values? How can we encourage them to play by the rules and stick within societal and parental limits? The answer is threefold. First, we must model a moral lifestyle. Second, we must grab the "teachable moment" that helps them see the reasons behind the rules. Third, we must call them out when they step beyond the boundaries.

We cannot overestimate the value of modeling behaviors and attitudes before our grandchildren. Nowhere is this more important than in the area of personal morality. As our grandsons and granddaughters make their way through the years of middle-childhood, they are slowly putting together a system of values. They do this in large part by watching how the significant adults in their lives act in key situations. That means our grandchildren are watching us to figure out what is right and wrong, and that can be pretty scary. The old saying that "your talk talks and your walk talks, but your walk talks louder than your talk" is true—especially with middle-years grandchildren.

Fairness is a major issue with children this age. Listen to them, and you will hear their conversation punctuated again and again with cries of, "That's not fair!" When we fail to walk our talk, our grandchildren may not say it aloud, but inside they are crying out, "That's not fair. You make me live by one set of rules and you follow another. It's just not fair!" Our grandchildren will see the inconsistencies. Just as a batter becomes angry at an umpire who moves the strike zone around, so our grandchildren will become angry when we say one thing and do another. We cannot hold them to standards of morality that we don't adhere to ourselves. It doesn't work to say, "Do as I say, not as I do." Grandchildren will end up doing what we do, regardless of what we say.

Our biggest concern with our middle-years grandchildren is that they take steps to follow Jesus during this formative time. More than anything else, I want my grandchild to learn obedience to Christ. To help them do that, I must make sure they see me live that way. I can talk about God all I want, but if my grandchildren don't see me back it up with my life, it will be to no avail. They'll know it isn't real. We pray every day that we will live consistently for Christ in front of our grandchildren. We ask God to help us as we try to live like Jesus before them.

Our second role as an umpire is to help our grandchildren see the purposes behind the rules and the reasons behind our values. We do this by taking advantage of every teachable moment we can. When they are with us, we have opportunities to use incidents and experiences to illustrate why there are rules and limits on behavior. A pastor took his grandson with him on an out-of-town speaking engagement. On the way home, they stopped at an unfamiliar restaurant and ordered dinner. Before it arrived, a man seated near them began to get obnoxious. His voice grew louder, and soon he was yelling obscenities. The man was drunk. The boy was about 10 years old at the time, and he had never seen an intoxicated man this close before. He listened and watched, then asked, "Why is that guy doing that, Grandpa?"

"Because he's drunk. He doesn't have control of himself." The boy looked at his grandfather and said, "Now I know why you don't ever want me to drink."

They talked for the next half hour about God's view of self-control and what the Bible says about drunkenness. That was a teachable moment, and the boy was able to see the reasons behind the rules.

If our grandchildren don't see those reasons but instead see rules as arbitrary and unfair, they will fight them. They may continue to struggle as they move on into high school and adulthood.

Teachable moments come often. Not all of them are as obvious as the one above, but each one gives us a chance to explain the need for values and the reasons behind the rules. We can grab those moments and use them to help our grandchildren complete their developmental tasks.

Our final responsibility as umpires is to call our grandchildren into account when they need it. I'm not talking about discipline here, but rather the gentle nudging of a developing conscience. When they err, we must not look at our grandchildren as if they had just committed the unpardonable sin. Instead, we should gently guide them back into right behavior and thinking. Unlike baseball umpires who scream at the top of their lungs, "YER OOOUUUTTT!" grandparent umpires whisper into the ear of their grandchildren, "Hey, look where you're standing. I think you're out of bounds."

Lauren is in her middle-childhood years. She is sometimes difficult to deal with. She is always pushing at the boundaries and questioning them. She needs to be reminded often that she is out of bounds, that she has two strikes and is in danger of swinging and missing again. Sometimes her grandpa wants to holler, "YER OUT!" because her actions have upset him or are bothering him. But when he looks at how fragile she is, and remembers that she is just learning about making the right decision, he tones it down. He slides up alongside her and says so no one can hear, "You're stepping out of bounds." It's usually enough for her to see that she has moved outside the lines. By treating her with respect and letting her keep her dignity when he calls her out, he enables her to maintain her self-esteem while building her values and morality.

The years of middle-childhood are vital to the growth and development of our grandchildren. Helping them complete their developmental tasks during these years is a high calling and a tall order. But we can do it. We can help our grandchildren build a sense of competence and self-sufficiency. Creative grandparents are just the right people to help children in the years of middle-childhood to find confidence and develop life skills. As a counselor, I have seen grandparents work the miracles in building the self-esteem of their grandchildren. I know it works. I've watched seven-year-old blue eyes light up when their grandparents become their number-one fans. I've seen children blossom under the gentle, yet firm imposition of fair limits and rules. I've watched patient, loving grandparents carefully explain the purpose behind those rules to their children. I have enjoyed watching grandparents model the Christian ethic consistently and with integrity.

Yes, we can help our grandchildren achieve the developmental tasks of this stage: industry and competence. We can help them overcome their feelings of inferiority. But it takes a creative plan. It takes our willingness to understand our middle-years grandchildren, and then to become their *coaches, cheerleaders,* and *umpires.*

List for creative grandparents
Here are five skills I have that I could teach my middle-years grandchild to do:

1.

2.

3.

4.

5.

Ten suggestions for activities that can give you the opportunity to become coach, cheerleader, *and* umpire *to a middle-years grandchild:*

1. Attend their games, matches, recitals, and concerts.
2. Take them to good movies or plays, then talk about them.
3. Watch their favorite television show with them and discuss it.
4. Take them with you for a weekend to the forest or lake shore.
5. Attend college or professional athletic events with them.
6. Let them teach you a new game and play it with them.
7. Take them backpacking.
8. Repair or build something with them.
9. Plant a flower or vegetable garden with them and tend it.
10. Go into business together making bows or painting sweatshirts.

Chapter Three

Time With Teenagers

Lynn was in tears. Only sixteen years old, and her life was falling apart. At least that's how she felt as she walked up to the front walk of Grandma's house. No one at school cared about her or even really knew her. All her friends had turned out to be phonies. They were more concerned that she wore the right clothes than how she was feeling inside. Even her parents had turned against her. They complained constantly about her grades and her social life, saying things like:

"Why don't you bring your friends over more often?"

"Lynn, you're living like a hermit. What's wrong with you?"

"Your grades are very disappointing this semester. We know you can do better. If they don't improve over the next marking period, we're going to have to take your car away from you."

Lynn knew that her grades were poor. But couldn't her parents see that she was doing the best she could? And how could she explain her feelings to her mother? Even though she was living through what were supposed to be the best years of her life, she felt desperate and alone.

Lynn was crying when she opened the familiar oak door that led into her Grandmother's home. "Lynn, what's the matter? Come on in. I'm glad to see you. I was wondering this morning how you were doing. I was just about to stop for a cup of coffee. Let me pour you one too, and we'll find out what's wrong."

Perhaps it was the familiar smell of baking and fresh coffee. Maybe it was the understanding she heard in her grandmother's voice. It may have been because Grandma never talked down to her, but treated her as an equal. It could be that she offered coffee rather than Coke, and she treated her problems with gravity and seriousness. It might have been the laugh-lines around her mouth, or her timeworn hands.

Whatever it was, Lynn was at ease. Her feelings tumbled out in a jumbled rush of words. Then her tears were gently wiped away by those loving hands. And even though her problems were not gone when she left Grandma's kitchen, they had become manageable again. It was as if her grandmother's six-and-a-half decades somehow had put her teenage difficulties into perspective. Looking into that deeply lined face, Lynn understood that life had not always treated Grandma gently either. After a little while with Grandma, Lynn felt that she would be able to withstand even the most difficult times.

Lynn's grandmother really didn't feel very special. She did not realize how important she was to her granddaughter. But her role in Lynn's teenage years was unique and extremely valuable.

Being a teenager is both wonderful and terrifying. It is wonderful to grow into a strong young man or lovely young woman. It's great to get that first job and first driver's license. Yet it can be terrifying to learn how to deal with your budding sexuality, to grow faster or not as fast as your peers, or to be shaking inside when everyone else seems calm and completely together.

It's tough to be a teenager in the nineties. Hard choices must be made and those decisions can alter a life forever. Today's adolescents are being pulled in a hundred directions. Commercials are saying, "Buy this soft drink or wear this brand of clothes and you'll be acceptable." Parents are pushing for good grades and career decisions. Peers are partying, drinking, and having sex. Adolescence constantly ask themselves, *Which voices should I listen to? Who is right? Which way should I go?*

The task of adolescence

The primary task of adolescence is to form a sense of identity. During the teen years, young people differentiate between themselves and their parents. They define and identify their own values, beliefs, and goals. Between the ages of twelve and eighteen they develop a sense of self.

In addition, teenagers are doing something for the first time that we grandparents have been doing for years—thinking abstractly. These "formal operations" begin in the early stages of adolescence. "Formal operations" is the ability to think abstractly; to think in terms of concepts and ideas. It is the ability to compare and decide, to make value-laden choices. And learning how to do that can be traumatic.

When Jack was eleven he was bright, enthusiastic, funny, and enjoyable to be around. He liked church and seeing his friends there. He would often hug his dad and give his mom a kiss, telling them that he loved them. But by age fourteen, Jack was not the same boy. He went from bright to overbearing, from enthusiastic to loud, from fun-loving to sarcastic, from enjoyable to surly.

The difference was "formal operations." Jack was beginning to think for himself. He was sorting out his values from his parents. He was also comparing them with his mental image of the ideal parents. Needless to say, they fell well short. It was a difficult time for Mom and Dad. They worried about the kind of person Jack was going to become. That's all part of adolescence.

Grandparenting teenagers like Jack can be frustrating and intimidating. But it can also be exciting and rewarding. Too bad so many grandparents simply stop trying to be involved with their adolescent grandchildren, choosing to wait until they "grow out of it."

Young children see their grandparents as gift-givers and playmates. But when those children reach their teen years, that role concept changes. Teens struggle with basic life questions. "Who am I?" they ask themselves. "Where do I fit in?" Facing these questions may cause them to distance themselves from their grandparents. Quite frankly, many teenagers don't appreciate anyone telling them how to live. Our gifts and antics, which they once saw as special or amusing, now strike them as corny and childish. No more trips to the zoo or playground. Grandparenting teenagers, therefore, requires greater effort, more discretion, and more tact than grandparenting younger children.

Don't let that scare you away from being the creative, involved grandparent of a teenager. True, grandparenting teens can be more work than it is for children, but it can be equally rewarding. Teenagers have a profound need to be loved and accepted unconditionally. Creative grandparents are especially good at doing just that. Teenagers also need a sense of continuity, of connection with the past, and Grandma is a walking history lesson. Teenagers need to develop interests and skills that establish uniqueness and identity, and grandparents have a lifetime of experience and a variety of abilities to draw from.

Creative grandparents of teenagers must assume four important roles if they are to help their grandchildren get through the confusing, crucial, formative years of adolescence: *teacher, family historian, facilitator,* and *friend.*

As *teachers,* creative grandparents can pass on the wisdom and skills acquired and honed over a lifetime. They can take the time to teach their grandchildren how to bake an apple pie or build a birdhouse. They can tell them how to apply for a job, use and take care of tools, or patch up a strained relationship.

As *family historians,* creative grandparents connect their grandchildren with the past and give them a feeling of continuity. Teenagers struggle to build a sense of identity. Unless they understand where they came from and how they fit in, they will have difficulty deciding where they want to go.

As *facilitators,* creative grandparents communicate to their grandchildren what Mom and Dad were like when they were teenagers. This clears the way for deeper understanding between parents and teens. When they hear about the foibles and ill-starred adventures of their parents, teenagers find it easier to identify with and understand them. When they learn of their accomplishments, they feel pride and are challenged themselves. They see Mom and Dad more completely and more realistically.

As *friends,* creative grandparents provide what teenagers consistently say is their deepest need—acceptance and love. They need them most when they do the things that are least acceptable, and when they are the most unlovable.

Grandparents as teachers

The woods were cold and silent. From the blind deep in the forest, Ed could hear the wind make its way through the stand of pines off to his left. A crunch in the snow snapped his attention forward, where a black squirrel was scurrying from tree to tree. A muffled yawn broke the stillness. Ed saw that Kyle, his fourteen-year-old grandson, was struggling to get fully awake. "What's wrong, Kyle? Was getting up at 5:30 too early for you?"

"It sure was, Grandpa. I can hardly stay awake."

"Do you want to go back to camp?"

"No. I'm a little sleepy, but I'm not going back. I've been wanting to do this since I was a little kid. No way I'm chickening out now."

Ed chuckled to himself. He thought back to when Kyle was a little boy begging to go deer hunting with Grandpa. "You can go when you're fourteen, Kyle. I promise."

"But I'm never going to be fourteen, Grandpa. That's a hundred years away."

Kyle did grow up, of course. Ed often wondered how the years could fly by so fast. It was wonderful to have the boy with him this brisk November morning for his first deer hunt. He had shown Kyle how to build a blind. He had given him lessons in reading deer sign. He had taught him how to shoot calmly and accurately.

Ed's reverie was broken by a crunch, and a flash of brown and white. It was unmistakably a white-tailed deer. "Kyle, look over there," he whispered urgently. Kyle rustled as he turned around in the blind. "Grandpa, it's a deer! Is it a buck?"

"Sure is, Kyle. Look at that rack! Okay now, line him up in your sights. No quick movements."

"But Grandpa, you saw him first." Kyle whispered hoarsely.

"I've shot plenty of deer in my lifetime, Kyle. Today it's your turn. Shhh. Put your scope on him and follow him in your sights. Do you see him?"

"Yeah. I see his antlers. They're huge!"

"All right. Take a deep breath and let it out slow. Aim just behind his shoulder. Pull easy. Don't jerk the trigger."

CRACK! The report of the rifle reverberated through the woods. "Grandpa, he went down. I got him!"

"Good shot, Kyle. Now let's go find him and clean him out. Looks like your Mom's going to have to learn how to cook venison."

"That was awesome, Grandpa!"

Ed watched happily as his ecstatic grandson ran to the animal.

A week or so later, relaxing in his recliner, Ed reflected over his many deer hunts. This was his most satisfying ever—and he never fired a shot!

It was a very special moment between a teenage boy and his grandfather. As teacher, Ed filled a need in Kyle's life. He passed on interests and skills that had been handed down in the family for generations. It gave him the opportunity to share a special, memorable moment with his adolescent grandson. And Ed's grandson revered him for his knowledge of the outdoors and his wealth of stories and experiences.

Filling the role of teacher can be a source of great satisfaction to a grandparent. Rarely will you feel more needed than when your granddaughter, just blossoming into womanhood, looks up at you from the garden and asks, "What do we plant next, Grandma, carrots or radishes?" Teenagers need to become proficient at something. They need to be able to point with pride and say, "I did that," or "You'll never believe what I did yesterday!" Gaining a skill fills a need to be good at something, to be different from everyone else without having to step out into bizarre nonconformity.

You may be asking yourself, "What do I have to offer my teenage grandchildren?" How about a lifetime of acquired skills? What are you good at? Do you sew? Teach your grandchild how. (The boys might want to learn— it's a new world.) Do you fish? Take your fifteen-year-old princess out for a couple hours on the lake. Do you work with wood? Can you draw? Paint? Do you collect anything? What skills have you learned through your vocation? Were you a nurse or a secretary? A tool-and-die man or a construction worker? It doesn't matter. You probably have a skill your grandchild would like to try.

As they teach, however, creative grandparents need to keep a few things in mind. Don't insist that your teenage grandson learn to play the viola just because you loved it when you were a kid. Remember the advice from chapter two: *follow their agenda*. That principle holds true for adolescents as well as toddlers. Let them choose. If they are interested in something you know nothing about, guide them to someone who does know—or take a crash-course yourself!

The only way to discover what your grandchildren would like to learn is to listen to them. Not just once, not just for a few minutes, but repeatedly and often. Some teenagers are afraid to reveal their personal thoughts. Even such an innocent desire as, "I'd really like to learn to sail like Grandpa," can remain a painfully guarded secret. The reason? These longings are closely tied to their identity, and adolescents are not about to let just anyone into their souls.

Teaching your teenage grandchildren will take perseverance, creativity, energy, and love. The return on the investment, however, is incredible. As creative, teaching grandparents, you can be one of the few welcomed into the inner life of a teenager—all because you shared a special knowledge or skill that helped your grandchild build personal identity.

Grandparents as family historians

Whenever an elderly person dies, a library burns down. This old saying is true. As people grow older, they accumulate knowledge of the past. When they are gone, that knowledge goes with them. Creative grandparents can be veritable libraries of history, especially family history. Our role is to remember what has gone before; to know everyone who did something important or embarrassing, and why.

This fits perfectly into the teenager's task of identity formation. It helps with the questions, "Who am I?" and "Who do I want to be?" One reason today's teens are struggling so mightily with the task of forming an identity is that they have lost a sense of connection with their families. They feel no continuity with the past. Researchers have different theories about the reasons for this, but they agree on one important point. If teenagers are to form a healthy sense of identity, they need to know where they came from and how they fit in. Creative historian grandparents connect them with the past and provide them with the continuity they are longing for.

As the librarians of family history, grandparents are much like the typical school library: neglected. Our teenage grandchildren have to be enticed to use us. Just as the teenager with the important research paper does not necessarily spend her evenings in the library, so the teenager in search of identity needs motivation to use her grandparents. As creative grandparents, we will have to motivate our grandchildren to learn family history from us.

How, you may ask, do we accomplish that? The cliché answer is, "Very carefully." But I'm not being flippant. Dealing with teens requires patience and perseverance. You might start by giving snippets from the past when the situation calls for it. You don't force history on anyone.

Christmas might be a good time to begin. "I remember Christmas Day, 1951. I had cold C-rations for dinner. Pretty near froze to death. Almost got shot."

What grandson could resist asking, "Grandpa, what was the deal? Where were you?"

"I was in Korea, John. We were fighting the communists of North Korea. I thought I was at least a hill or two away from the enemy. So I walked around, kind of carelessly. But the North Koreans reminded me that communists don't believe in Christmas by using me for target practice. As I dove for cover, I thought, *You idiot! Don't you know any better?*"

Sharing tidbits of historical information will catch the imagination of your grandchildren and may leave them asking for more. "He was the most incredible looking guy I ever saw! Jill, I know you girls today think you invented hunks. But Mike Rogers was the prototype, at least for me. Really turned me on."

"Grandma, I can't believe you said that!"

"What do you mean 'said that'? Of course I said that. He was a hunk."

"Grandma, you felt like that about guys and stuff?"

"Of course I did, Jill. I was young once too."

As grandparents relate the pieces of the story every family has, their teenagers will begin to feel a sense of their place in the world. They will start to understand what went on before they came along, and how they fit into the picture. It makes their task of building identity far easier. Without them even being aware of it, you will have helped your grandchildren accomplish the most important task of adolescence.

As family historians, you would be wise to follow these guidelines:

1. Tell the truth! That may seem obvious, but truth can be slippery and difficult to maintain. We are tempted to leave out stuff that is, well, embarrassing or indecorous. Yet Ephesians 4:25 warns us to "put off falsehood and speak truthfully." Grandparents who edit the family history to protect certain sensibilities are hurting their grandchildren. A fourteen-year-old girl is reassured to know that her grandmother had a huge crush on a cute guy in the ninth grade, but that she never found a way to tell him she liked him. It helps for Grandpa to tell that he got a D in algebra, and that he never really did like gym class. It brings them closer, and it helps teens identify with their grandparents.

The temptation is always there to make things better or worse than they actually were for the sake of the story. Resist the temptation to create heroes. Your grandchildren should be able to count on you to tell the truth. If you do go off into a tall-tale (and I feel that's always your right as a grandparent), find a way to let them know where truth ended and fiction began.

2. Allow for an MTV attention span. Grandparents must realize that many teenagers today have restless

minds that flit from one thought to the next. It is increasingly difficult, especially for young adolescents, to con-
centrate for long periods of time. These are people
weaned on cartoons and used to watching sitcoms or
music videos, where the picture changes every three to
five seconds, and where they are never more than eight
minutes from a commercial. Talking three hours straight
just will not work for them. Tell the family history in
short episodes, not as a *Roots* mini-series.

3. *Ask for a response.* Help your teenager get involved
in the story. You might ask if they have ever wanted to
do something like that, or if they have ever felt that way.
Once they start talking, let them go on. You are getting
valuable inside information. Remember, telling the family history is a means to an end. The goal is identity formation, and a growing trust between grandparent and
teenager is a valuable by-product.

4. *Weave your faith in Christ into the story.* If you are a
Christian family, a history that excludes God is incom-
plete. Teenagers need to know that faith works. They
need to know that it is possible to live as a child of God
in spite of very real human failings. Fill your history with
the story of God's love. Tell them how His hand was on
your life. Don't force it. Don't preach your faith to them.
Just say it with the conviction of your heart.

One grandmother received Christ at a small country
church when she was still a girl. Years later, she vividly
described the music, the preacher, and the one who
prayed with her to receive Jesus. She told how her faith
helped carry her through the long, tough days of the
Great Depression. Her granddaughter listened carefully.
Her grandmother did not know that she was struggling
with an important decision. The grandmother's story of

faith eventually led her granddaughter to obey Christ on a critical issue—and to lead her children into following Him as well.

Grandparents as facilitators

"I think the best thing about Grandma is the way she tells stories about Dad. She tells me what he was like and what he did when he was my age." These words from a fifteen-year-old girl describe the role of facilitator that creative grandparents can assume.

Adolescence can be a time of strain between parents and children. Even the strongest, most loving families go through difficulties when their children become teenagers. When our son Jack was sixteen, he challenged us constantly. He was always testing to see how far he could push out the boundaries. Jack was not a bad kid, not at all. He was normal. We were not bad parents. We were normal. But our normal reactions sometimes created friction, and friction can erupt into anger and arguments.

During these years, Jack often went over to visit my father (usually to pay back money he had borrowed). Now, Jack could have mailed him the money. But talking to Grandpa and Grandma Schreur was special: it meant getting the lowdown on Dad.

My mother and dad would relate the struggles they had with me when I was a teenager. I was a rebellious teen, always in trouble. I was in and out of jail. I drove recklessly and fast. Hearing about this from his grandparents made a deep impact on Jack. My mother wept as she told about her wayward son, wondering if I would kill myself or someone else in my car, or get shot by the police. As she talked, Jack was deciding that he was not going to put his mother through the same thing.

As Jack and I were writing this book, he told me that listening to my parents' stories helped him better understand me and my parenting style. My parents had become facilitators, helping my son understand me.

Some parents are not willing to let their teenagers see them as real people. Perhaps they are afraid of losing control or respect. As creative grandparents, we can tactfully bridge that gap, not by interfering, but by honestly telling it like it was.

Two dangers must be avoided by grandparents as facilitators:

1. We must not use this role to get back at our children for unresolved conflicts.

2. We are not to use it to manipulate our grandchildren or undermine their parents.

If we have unresolved hurts or struggles with our grown children, we must resolve those issues with them. Grandparents must never use their grandchildren as weapons in a power play. Teenagers are too fragile and too precious to be misused in that manner! Please be careful. It's all too easy to fall into this trap. We are telling about our children, not to get even with them, but to help them and their teenagers understand one another.

Just as important, we must not misuse the facilitator role by manipulating our grandchildren into an "us versus them" mode—us against their parents. We are striving to bring understanding, not discord. We must speak about their parents with the highest respect, and we must support their decisions. We also need to let our children know what we are telling our grandchildren about them and why. This will prevent misunderstanding and suspicion.

One grandparent told his grandson about the great disappointment in his father's life. He had wanted to go to college to study architecture, but the war and finances prevented it. That seemed to give the boy direction, and it helped him understand his father. The young man later graduated from Purdue as an architectural engineer. He fulfilled his father's dream, and he found great satisfaction in his career.

As facilitators, creative grandparents strive for better understanding between parents and teens. While we are building that understanding, we are also drawing them into a vital relationship that adds enjoyment to our lives and strengthens their personal identity and connection with the past.

Grandparents as friends

Most grandparents want at least to be familiar with their teenage grandchildren. Yet the role many desire most is that of friend. Fulfilling that desire can be slow, difficult, even impossible. We want from our adolescent grandchildren an open, trusting relationship, but they do not always want the same from us.

Consider Sarah, a vital, energetic, sixty-five-year-old grandmother. Her five grandchildren are just about the dearest things in her world to her. Sarah is troubled about her oldest grandson, Adam. He is fourteen, and he doesn't want to be around her anymore. Although she seldom lets it show, she is crushed by his refusal to come near her or let her kiss him.

Sarah felt terrible on the family's annual vacation trip to Florida over spring break. In previous years they had played games together in the motor home. They were silly traveling games mostly, like "slugbug" and "most states on license plates." But on this trip Adam sat sullenly in the corner and stared blankly out the window—all the way to Florida. Once they got there, he wasn't much better. Adam was always trying to get away from the family and go off on his own. He even refused to go for ice cream with Sarah, a long-standing vacation tradition.

When the trip was over, Sarah told her story and asked, "What did I do wrong? What can I do to get Adam back?" The answers: Nothing. And wait. Adam is simply being an early adolescent.

While forming that all-important sense of identity, teenagers need distance and freedom. Sometimes we are sure that they are cutting themselves off from the family, but that is usually not the case. They are lengthening the cords. And the reason is no mystery. Even though teenagers need to feel connected, they also need to find out who they are apart from their families. This process can leave Mom and Dad frustrated and bewildered. The same is true of grandparents who love that teenage grandchild and want to be his friend. These grandparents must recognize that they are not being rejected. They can still have a deep and meaningful relationship with their teenage grandson. But it must be on his terms.

Three principles for becoming friends with your teenage grandchildren are: wait, accept, shelter. Let's look at each of them.

1. Wait. To wait for our grandchildren is to give them the time and space they need to figure out who they are and who they will become. If we demand closeness now, we will drive them away—perhaps forever. We must be patient and persevering, waiting for them to come back to us. Grandchildren usually create this sense of distance between the ages of twelve to fifteen. Then, from ages sixteen to eighteen, they gradually close the gap again. Younger adolescents are still working through their task of identity formation, while the older ones have become secure enough in themselves to inch back into a close relationship with Grandma and Grandpa.

Older adolescents often want friendship with their grandparents. We must realize that by waiting, we are letting them grow up. When they come back, they do so as "almost adults." Because of their newfound reasoning skills and maturity, along with a growing self-confidence, they are more delightful to be with than when they left. They distance themselves as anguished children and return as young adults.

Be patient. Let them do what they have to do. And above all—don't give up on them too soon.

2. Accept. Do teenagers ever feel completely accepted? Television commercials push them to aspire for the perfect body, the perfect hair, the perfect face. As our teenagers compare themselves with the images on the flickering screen, they are left with the undeniable impression that they are not good enough. Because adolescents are struggling through deep issues of image and self-esteem, they are vulnerable to exploitation. Some teens will do just about anything for that feeling of safety and security that accompanies acceptance. This "fitting in" process can be as simple and harmless as a weird hairstyle or an absurdly expensive pair of sneakers. Sometimes it's deadly, involving alcohol, lawlessness, sexual activity, and drug abuse.

Creative grandparents can accomplish wonders with their teenage grandchildren by accepting them for who they are and loving them regardless of their behavior. This, of course, does not involve condoning destructive or immoral behavior. What we must communicate to them is that our love and acceptance is unconditional. That's pretty difficult, of course, when they've got blue spiked hair. But remember, your acceptance is not based on what they do, but on who they are.

Think about it. Adolescents live in a performance-oriented world. They are valued for how well they do things. Get good grades, Mom and Dad accept you. Have the right look, and your peers accept you. Be a starter on the basketball team, and the community accepts you. In each of these circumstances, however, the teen is being valued for what he can do instead of for who he is.

This factor has dangerous implications for self-esteem and identity formation. The adolescent quickly learns that his feelings are really not very important to most people; it's how well he performs that counts. The important thing is to succeed—no matter what the cost. This in itself drives some teenagers into self-destructive or immoral behavior. So does repeated failure.

Creative grandparents come to their teenagers with an established, tested set of values. They communicate to their grandchildren that their love is unconditional. It is not based on outward appearance or achievements, but on relationship. "You are my granddaughter. I will love you forever, regardless of your success or failure, your appearance, or your actions. To me you are always beautiful, and you are always mine. And I'm glad and proud to claim you as my granddaughter."

A true story will illustrate. Matt was an excellent athlete and a good student. He was popular with the other teenagers and accepted by everyone. But then he got thrown off the basketball team for drinking. Suddenly his friends on the team didn't have time for him. His parents were disappointed with him. Soon Matt felt alone, rejected by everyone.

Later he described the important role his grandparents played during this critical period with these words: "My grandfather and grandmother never stopped caring about me. After school, while my friends were at basketball practice, I would feel very down and alone. So I walked over to Grandpa's and Grandma's house. Grandma never yelled at me about the drinking. She knew that I knew it was a stupid thing to do. Instead, she listened to me as I talked about anything and everything. She and Grandpa were the only ones who did not treat me differently after I got thrown off the team. They, especially Grandma, loved me all the way through it."

This is creative grandparenting at its best! It provides a listening ear and unqualified acceptance to adolescents working through this very cold, uncaring world.

3. *Shelter.* The Old Testament emphasizes a concept that personifies creative grandparenting. In Israel there were six cities of refuge (Joshua 20). If an Israelite accidentally killed someone, he could flee to these cities for safety. Tribal law and custom demanded that someone who killed another be killed in return: "A life for a life." But this was not fair in the case of an accident. To protect the innocent, God established cities of refuge throughout Israel. Someone who accidentally took the life of another could go for there for refuge. The people of the city were obligated to protect him.

As creative grandparents, we want to befriend and help our grandchildren through the teenage years. One thing we can do is turn our house into a "city of refuge" for them. We can provide a place for them out of harm's way. We can protect them and offer them safe keeping. The Bible describes it this way:

> When [the accidental slayer] flees to one of these cities, he is to stand in the entrance of the city gate and state his case before the elders of that city. Then they are to admit him into their city and give him a place to live with them. If the avenger of blood pursues him, they must not surrender the one accused . . . (Josh. 20:4).

Creative grandparents are sanctuaries; our homes are cities of refuge to our adolescent grandchildren. We offer them a place they can flee to when it feels as though the world is crashing down around them. I have an image of myself standing at the city gate and telling my granddaughter's pursuers, "Stop! I have her now. She is safe here. You cannot harm her anymore." Then those seeking to harm my granddaughter turn away empty-handed.

Creating a safe atmosphere will endear your teenage grandchildren to you forever. They need a place of refuge, a sanctuary. You can provide it. And in so doing you can teach them about God, who is their fortress and strength through all of life (Ps. 27:1).

As creative grandparents, we can be friends with our teenage grandchildren. But we must be willing to wait for them to come to us. We must not push them into a relationship they do not desire. We must always be available to them. We must accept them for who they are, knowing that teens often struggle with low self-esteem and feelings of inferiority. We can communicate an unconditional love that does not fade with time or distance. Grandparents who wish to be friends with their teenage grandchildren can become cities of refuge in a cold and hostile world. Our homes can be sanctuaries in the storms, lighthouses in the darkness, places of safety and love for our struggling adolescent grandchildren.

A *homework assignment!*

Grandparenting through the teenage years can be difficult and frustrating. That is the nature of relationships with teenagers. We can play an important role in their lives during these critical years. We can help them with their main job, identity formation. We can do that creatively by assuming the roles of teacher, family historian, facilitator, and friend.

One more suggestion for grandparenting teens. Take time to read about adolescence. Learn what they are like and what they are going through. Understanding adolescents makes it a whole lot easier to be sympathetic with them, even when they are not acting responsibly. We suggest you purchase David Elkind's easy-to-read book, *All Grown Up and No Place to Go*. Taking a few weeks of your life to do a little reading will enable you to become a far better grandparent during the six years of your grandchild's adolescence.

You could end up like Lynn's grandmother. She taught Lynn about faith, about dealing with fears by facing them, and even about boys. She did all of that without even realizing what she was doing. She was simply loving her precious granddaughter. She just accepted Lynn and provided a place of refuge for her. Now, years later, Lynn still gets a lump in her throat when she talks about her grandmother. "Grandma changed my life," she says. "So many times when I was alone, she was my friend. I could not have made it without her. And I bet she never knew it."

I bet, deep down inside, she did!

Chapter Four

When the Family Is Falling Apart

It was one of those calls every parent dreads—the stuff of sleepless nights and agonizing days. "Dad, Mom, this is Rebecca. I'm over at Patty's house. Something is wrong. Could you please come over right away? I'd rather wait until you get here to tell you about it."

For Pam and Mike, the drive down the familiar road to daughter Patty's house seemed endless. They couldn't help but wonder what was happening. Was Rebecca or Patty sick? Or could it be that four-month-old grandson Jason, the joy of their lives, had suddenly become ill? When they walked through the door of their oldest daughter's home, Pam caught her breath. It was obvious that their two daughters had been crying. Pam's eyes roved the room, searching for Jason's bassinet. Relief at seeing him sleeping peacefully in the corner overwhelmed her. She was not aware how concerned she had been. But what was wrong?

Rebecca spoke quietly. "Patty, maybe you'd better tell them yourself."

"Tell us. What's wrong? We're worried sick. We thought something had happened to Jason."

Patty tried to speak, but her voice broke. Finally she blurted out, "Mom, Dad, I can't believe this is happening to me." The words were gushing out now, like water. "James came home from work Friday and he said . . . he said . . . he's been seeing another woman."

"What do you mean? Was he telling you that he is having an affair?"

"Yes! And, Oh, Dad, he's been seeing her for more than a year. I don't know what to do. He wants a divorce. This isn't really happening. It can't be! Mom, he loves me. At least he is supposed to. I mean, the whole time I was pregnant with Jason, he was sleeping with her." Patty's body shook.

Mike looked around. Rebecca was crying. He wondered if he were really there, if it were all some sort of sick joke. But he knew it was not. He felt an air of unreality at being called away from a normal supper on a normal day and being told this kind of news. His son-in-law was unfaithful to his oldest daughter. And she was in deep pain and shock.

Mike glanced at his sleeping grandson. The infant was unaware of the hard turn his life had taken. Mike was not one to show his emotions, but he buried his head in his burly hands and cried. He wept for the hurt to his daughter. He wept for the uncertainty of his grandchild's future. He wept for the shattering of his own dreams.

It wasn't supposed to be like this. He and Pam had been good parents. They had raised their children in the church. They had instilled in them good values by teaching and example. His daughters had grown to be mature, attractive Christian women. They had married, purchased homes, borne children. Life was good. Everything seemed perfect—until this. Mike wondered how everyone would be affected now that his daughter's family appeared to be falling apart. Is it too late? Is reconciliation still possible? Life had taken a difficult turn indeed. It would never be quite the same.

During a time of family crisis, grandparents carry a special responsibility and burden. We can help our children through the crisis. We can be an invaluable resource to our children and grandchildren during the dark and stressful days. Crisis often strikes without warning. It leaves no time for preparation. Mike and Pam's experience is common. Many families have experienced similar heartbreak. One moment the world is revolving on its axis and all is well; the next, it seems to have careened off-course and is spinning wildly out of control.

In this chapter we will think together about how grandparents can be a help and resource during four common crises of life their children may face: divorce, chronic illness, death, and disability. No one can ever really be ready for these eventualities. Sometimes we're afraid even to talk about them. But it still may occur. And if it does, creative, involved grandparents can be the difference between the family that handles the crisis successfully and the one that collapses under the strain and pressure. We can offer two things they need most: help and hope.

Grandparenting during divorce

With our society's divorce rate continuing to soar, many parents will have to watch at least one of their children go through the pain and trauma of divorce. Our purpose is not to debate the rightness or wrongness of divorce from a cultural or biblical perspective. Rather, we are approaching it as a sad reality of life in the latter half of the twentieth century. We want to show grandparents how they can creatively, constructively be involved in the lives of their children and grandchildren if divorce does occur. We strongly believe that grandparents can be a powerful help and source of hope during this traumatic experience.

When circumstances force you to grandparent during the divorce of one of your children, consider the following principles:

- Don't judge in haste.
- Make yourself and your resources available.
- Establish clear boundaries.
- Maintain contact.

Don't judge in haste. As Mike sat in his daughter's living room, he was overwhelmed with anger. How could his son-in-law behave that way? How could he have so little concern for his infant son? How could he just throw his marriage away? Mike felt a surge of anger. He wanted to find James and settle the score. He had not felt this way since he became a Christian many years before. With obvious effort to control his rage he asked, "Patty, where is your husband? Why isn't he here?" Mike's voice was controlled, steely, even though a fire burned hot inside him. His voice rose. "Patty, I want to talk to him. Tell me where he is. Now!"

"Dad, he's at work. He didn't want to be here when I told you. Please don't do something rash. It will only make things worse."

Mike paced the room. Then he and Pam did what they could to offer support to Patty and to reassure her of their continued love. On the way home, they talked. Mike's anger was subsiding and rationality had returned. As he expressed his feelings, Pam kept saying the same thing over and over again: "Mike, remember, we don't know everything that went on in that house. It's not fair to blame James entirely. Let's wait until we get the whole story."

Mike resisted her efforts to calm him down and get him to see both sides. He loved his daughter. He found it difficult to think that she might share some of the responsibility. After all, James was having the affair. Patty had been completely faithful.

The truth, however, was that Mike and Pam had foreseen difficulties in this relationship from the beginning. The shock was not that Patty and James were so near divorce, but that he had betrayed her. Even so, Pam's point was well taken. She and Mike would be able to help even more if they refrained from rushing into judgment.

A year-and-a-half later, Mike and Pam looked back at this difficult time. They were asked, "What advice would you give to parents during the divorce of their children?" Immediately, and almost in unison, they answered, "Don't be judgmental. It's almost impossible to avoid pinning the blame on someone, but you have to try."

Creative grandparents who want to be a force for good and a source of support during the marital difficulties of their children must continuously fight their own deeply ingrained loyalties. The natural tendency is to side immediately with our own flesh and blood. We direct all the anger we feel at the other person involved. Not only is this unfair, it may disrupt or destroy our relationships with our grandchildren.

Consider Marcy, whose grandchildren live with her divorced daughter. Marcy spends at least two afternoons a week with the children. She loves them and they love her. However, Marcy is deeply angry with her former son-in-law. Her daughter's divorce was unexpectedly bitter. The custody battle had been distasteful, with accusations and innuendo traded equally between combatants who, until recently, had been lovers and marriage partners. Every time she is with her grandchildren, Marcy cannot resist speaking against their father to them. She feels that the joint custody awarded by the court was a severe mistake, and she doesn't miss an opportunity to express her feelings to the children.

Marcy's rage and resentment have blinded her to the harm she is doing her grandchildren. She is putting them into a position where they have to choose who they are going to love, their father or their mother. Her grandchildren, only four and six, do not like her to watch them anymore. The anguish she causes in their half-formed psyches is too much for them. They love their mother and their father, and they still don't understand why they can't live together anymore. Grandma Marcy is making it even tougher on them to adjust and survive.

During the pain of divorce, everything in us cries out to make a snap judgment in defense of our children. We want to protect them, to justify their actions. But divorce is rarely a one-way street. Even in a situation that seems one-sided, such as an extramarital affair, the real difficulties often remain hidden. Most of the time an affair is a symptom of deeper issues, not the root cause. This is not to minimize the offense. But we must guard against becoming judge, jury, and executioner. At stake are things far more important than our personal sense of outrage: the possibility of reconciliation, the needs of our son or daughter, and the well-being of our grandchildren. For their sakes, and sometimes just to give the marriage a chance, we must keep our judgments to ourselves.

Make yourself and your resources available. During and after a divorce, we can provide a place of security and constant love for grandchildren who are afraid that they are going to lose one or both of their parents. This is another reason to withhold judgment. Now that Mom or Dad has moved out, those children will wonder if the one who left has stopped loving them. They may be afraid that the parent they are living with will go away too, leaving them alone.

For children struggling with these feelings, creative grandparents can offer a reliable refuge during the stormy proceedings of the divorce and aftermath. Mom and Dad may be preoccupied and angry, but Grandma can quietly assure the children that she will love them and be there for them. Sometimes the parents each try to enlist the children to their side in the divorce. The children are pulled by conflicting loyalties and confusing emotions. They do not need us to pressure them into taking sides; rather, they need us to be understanding and patient, providing them quiet support and constant love.

We will also help them immensely if we maintain a degree of objectivity when they ask us about the divorce. This is how the conversation might go.

"Grandma, why did Mommy take us away from Daddy? Why can't we live with him anymore?"

"That, my dear granddaughter, is a grown-up question. You must be growing up. The answer to some questions is hard to find, Megan. I don't always understand what happened between your mom and dad either. But I do know this: They both love you very much. Your daddy has promised that even though you aren't living together anymore, he will still see you often. Sometimes he will take you over to his house so you can stay with him."

"I know, Grandma, but why does Mom say mean things about Dad? Is he bad?"

"Honey, your mom is really feeling bad right now. Once she and your dad loved each other very much, but now they aren't so sure. This makes your mom sad. When people are sad, sometimes they say hard things. Do you do that sometimes?"

"Yes, Grandma, I do. Will they stop loving me sometime too?"

"No, Megan, they will not. You are their daughter, and just like I will never stop loving your mom, she will never, ever stop loving you. And I know your dad feels the same way. And Megan, you will always be my special girl, even though you are growing up way too fast."

We can be a valuable resource to our children and grandchildren if we will listen more than we talk. We must hear our children. We must hear the spouse. Of course, we must also listen to our grandchildren. We must let them tell us what they are thinking and feeling. Let them ask the difficult, "adult" questions. Let them express their fears. And when they do, we have to resist the temptation to provide simplistic responses or pat answers. Talk openly to them about the fact that both persons share the responsibility for most divorces. Be open about the deep feelings of ambiguity and pain that accompany a divorce. Don't express your anger at your child or the marital partner to your grandchildren. Turn the energy the anger generates into being the best, wisest, most loving grandparent you can be. If you waste it on anger or bitterness, you will accomplish nothing except to add further turmoil to your grandchildren's already confused lives.

Mike and Pam were now faced with a difficult decision. After seeing a family counselor and attempting to salvage her marriage, their daughter decided to file for divorce. But she had no place to stay, and the agreement said she had to be out of her husband's house within 90 days. Foreseeing this possibility, Mike and Pam had considered inviting their grown daughter and her infant son into their home. They weren't sure they were ready for that. Their lifestyle would have to change drastically. After being "on their own" for a number of years, they would be committing themselves to caring for a baby and their increasingly fragile daughter.

In the end, the decision was easy. There simply were no good alternatives. So they went to Patty together and asked her if she would temporarily move in with them. Relieved, Pat agreed, "Just for a few weeks, until I can afford an apartment." The few weeks stretched into months. And Pam and Mike found themselves involved in their grandson's life to an extent they had never anticipated. But later they saw it as a rewarding, fulfilling interlude in their lives.

During the stress of divorce, parents run low on two important resources: time and money. On an average, women's resources dip dramatically following a divorce, while men become responsible for child support. The result is a drain on everyone's financial resources. Although grandparents may not be affluent, they can be of help.

One grandparent we know realizes that her daughter will never ask her for money, even in desperation. So this grandmother takes her grandchildren shopping and purchases clothes for them. Her daughter's muted protests are met with, "It's a grandmother's prerogative." Her daughter chooses to accept that, and she appreciates keeping her dignity while her children are getting the clothes they need.

A grandfather takes his divorced son and his grandson out to dinner. He realizes that his son struggles with finances, and he knows that cooking day after day is not easy for him. So, a couple times a week, they go out to eat as a family.

Creative grandparents will see a lot of ways they can help their children or grandchildren when a divorce occurs. And they will find ways to do so without robbing their son or daughter of their dignity. For example, one parent provided the security deposit for his daughter's apartment after she and her husband divorced and she had to give up their home. It was $400 she just did not have. He let her know that he was doing it simply as an act of love, and she let him do it on that basis.

For your enjoyment and well-being as a parent, your involvement should be voluntary. You do not force it on your children; they do not take it for granted. If your children just assume that you will always come to the rescue, it will become a burden rather than a privilege. This is true of all the kinds of help you may be in position to give, including babysitting.

Offering your time may be an even more important way to help than giving money over the long run. Divorcing parents are under a great deal of stress. Finding a new place to live, getting a job, meeting with lawyers, appearing before the court, and negotiating the settlement may consume much of the time they have. The emotional drain is enormous. Creative grandparents will find ways to alleviate this strain.

Pam and Mike, for example, soon found themselves putting Jason to bed nearly every night. His mother, exhausted by stressful days of job-hunting and personal adjustment, was relieved when Mom and Dad volunteered to give Jason his bath and dress him for bed. Patty greatly appreciated Mom's offer to watch Jason while she looked for work, and assured her of assistance when she did find a job. When Patty needed a weekend away to sort out her thinking, do some healing, and look to the future, Pam and Mike volunteered to take care of Jason.

As creative grandparents in a divorce situation, take the time to think through the situation your child is in. Ask what you can do to give her the best help. Offer some suggestions you may have thought about. What do they need in financial help? How can it be done the easiest and least painful way? How can your available time be used to their best advantage? It may not be what you expect. Ask specific questions: "Would it help if I came over and watched the children for two hours every other morning?" "Would this be a good weekend to take the children?" This is the best way to discover what you can do to help during the difficult time of a divorce.

In chapter two we talked about inconveniencing ourselves to meet the needs of our wonder-years grandchildren. We need to be willing to do the same to help our children during a divorce, thereby helping our grandchildren as well.

To do this, we may first have to deal with the anger we feel toward our children for putting their kids in this position. Both spouses were probably at fault for the lack of success in the marriage. You may have even "seen it coming" and warned them. They may well have made some bad choices along the way to the divorce, choices you cautioned them about beforehand. You *must* remember that they probably already know that. Most people feel horrible about what is happening. They feel like failures, even though they may have done all they could to

make it work out. They do *not* need Mom or Dad telling
them how wrong, stupid, or immature they are. And
even if they are, all we will accomplish by telling them is
to alienate them when they need us the most. Deal with
your anger yourself. Don't fill your child's life with, "I
told you so's." Be available to them as a resource in this
time of crisis. See it as an opportunity to minister to your
child and grandchildren. They don't need your disgust;
they need your love and support.

You might want to encourage your child to seek the
help of a reputable Christian counselor. People experiencing severe marital problems need someone to help them
work objectively through their relationship. You may
have to urge them to consider counseling, but it just may
save the marriage. Even if they divorce, your child might
still benefit greatly from a Christian counselor's assistance.

Patty stayed with Pam and Mike for six months.
Grandma and Grandpa grew closer to Jason than they
ever thought possible. They fed him, bathed him, and
played with him. They helped him learn and watched
him grow. They held him when he cried and kissed away
his hurts. Pam and Mike point to their months of living
with little Jason and his mom as the primary reason for
the deep bonds that still exist between them. To be sure,
there were flare-ups. Sometimes Patty's expectations for
her parents were too high. On the whole, however, the
experience strengthened their relationship.

Pam and Mike supplied the place for Patty and Jason
to live, purchased all the food, occasionally babysat, and
included her in their lives for six months. By that time
she had saved enough money to get an apartment of her
own. When they were asked if they regretted anything,

Pam and Mike agreed on this: "We are sorry the divorce happened. We still hope and pray for reconciliation, though it doesn't seem likely. But we loved being with our daughter again. And we were delighted to be with Jason during those crucial months of his life and get to know him. We are better parents and grandparents because of this experience."

Establish clear boundaries. Mike and Pam struggled with what their role should be during this critical time. Sometimes they felt that they were parenting Jason. They neither wanted nor sought this role. Their daughter, who was struggling with her own feelings about herself, sometimes seemed to let them parent both her and her child.

Establishing clear boundaries between parenting and grandparenting is the third key to effective grandparenting during divorce. As we lend support and encouragement, and as we make our resources available to our children and grandchildren, everyone involved must understand that we are not becoming surrogate parents. Our role is completely different. We are there to lend support and love; we are not there to take over the job of parenting when our children are preoccupied and under great stress. We can assist them, but we must not replace them.

Grandparents must not enable their children to abandon their parental roles by allowing parental responsibility to slide over to themselves. Nor should they take it because they enjoy it. Many grandparents are eager to assume that role. But research shows that grandparents who take on the parenting responsibilities lose the sense of satisfaction, adventure, and fun that is so crucial to their well-being in the relationship. One grandparent expressed it this way: "I've already raised my children. I love my grandchildren, and I want to help my daughter through her divorce. But I'm not the child's parent, and I don't want to act like one. Besides, I don't know what my health will be like in a couple years."

We must draw the line sharply between parenting and grandparenting if we are going to grandparent successfully. The only way to achieve this is to let our children know exactly what we will do and what we feel is inappropriate. If we don't communicate this to our children, they won't know where the line is. They may wonder, for example, if it's okay for them to ask us to feed their children or put them to bed. They may wonder if we are beginning to resent having to do these tasks. Grandparents remove the ambiguity and uncertainty when they draw the boundaries realistically and clearly. Do not be afraid of hurting your daughter or son's feelings. The chances of hurt feelings are far more likely when our feelings are not made known clearly, lovingly, and precisely.

Maintain contact. Grandparents must remember that they have the right and responsibility to maintain contact with their grandchildren following a divorce. This can be especially difficult when custody has been awarded to the parent who is not their child. Grandparents often stop trying to see their grandchildren, giving up hope that they can be a presence and influence in their grandchild's life. But it does not have to be this way.

First of all, grandparents have a legal right to petition to visit their grandchildren. This is true even if a messy custody case has gone in favor of the other parent.

The courts have repeatedly stated that it in is the best interest of the child to have involvement with maternal and paternal grandparents. If you had a pre-divorce relationship with the grandchildren, you may be granted the right to see them even if the custodial parent does not wish it.

Grandparents will maintain contact much more easily if they establish a good relationship with the custodial parent. Earlier in the chapter, we urged grandparents to avoid taking sides and rushing to judgment. Keeping in contact with your grandchildren after the divorce is one reason for doing this. It is better for the children (and their parents) if you avoid establishing an antagonistic relationship. Otherwise the children once again are forced to handle severely divided loyalties. Do your best not to put them in that position.

Mothers are awarded custody in a majority of cases in the United States. If you are the paternal grandparent, do your best to maintain a loving relationship with the children's mother. Remember, blame usually can be assigned to both parents, and to the circumstances. By refusing to lay all the blame on your daughter-in-law, you improve the possibility of having a good relationship with her. And that will open the door to maintaining contact with your precious grandchildren.

Grandparents can be given legal rights to spend time with their grandchildren. More important, however, is their moral responsibility to maintain contact following a divorce—especially if they want to be an ongoing influence for the values of Christ.

Children whose grandparents have stayed in contact with them and have played an important role in their development are much less likely to have struggles and difficulties later. The research shows that it is usually "in the best interest of the child" to have continuing contact with the grandparents. The reason is clear: Involved grandparents help their grandchildren cope with the trauma of divorce and growing up afterward. Therefore, grandparents have a moral responsibility to help their grandchildren "grow up divorced." They need the stability and strength and love their grandparents can give them. Your grandchildren desperately need you, whether they recognize it or not. Don't let them down by failing to do your best to maintain contact, difficult though it may be.

When a family experiences a divorce, everyone suffers. It can be especially difficult for the children. They often feel alone and insecure. They are at the mercy of frightening forces they do not understand and cannot change. By not rushing to judgment, by making our resources available, by drawing clear boundaries, and by maintaining contact, we can offer these children the support they need.

Grandparenting during a family crisis

Judy can still feel her heart sinking into her stomach. She cannot forget the knot of nausea she felt as she drove from her office to the accident. Jack's call had been confusing. "Mom, I'm calling from somebody's car phone on I-96. We've been in an accident. Jonathon and Erin are all right. Can you come? Please hurry!" Looking back, Judy remembers wondering as she drove what life would be like without one of her grandchildren. How could she deal with that? How could she support Jack or Leslie if her own heart were broken?

She arrived at the scene just in time to watch the paramedics strap one-year-old Jonathon to a stretcher and slide him into an ambulance. His three-year-old sister Erin left next, then her son Jack. She prayed as she drove to the hospital, "Oh, God, please take care of them. Don't let them be hurt bad. Please, God, let them be all right. Please!"

The scene at the hospital was both alarming and reassuring. Erin and Jonathan were bruised and frightened, but news soon came that they were okay. Seatbelts had saved them from serious injury.

But Jack, who was driving when his car was struck at seventy miles-per-hour, was not doing so well. Chest x-rays showed a problem with his heart. The doctors spoke of "deceleration" and the need for "an immediate heart catheterization." Judy's joy at hearing the children were unhurt was swept aside by this troubling news. As she sat in the hospital with the family and friends, she felt terrified. What if he died? How do you grandparent children who have lost their father?

The silence was overwhelming. Jack had been gone for a long time. Just as the heaviness seemed unbearable, the doctor walked briskly in. "I think Jack's going to be okay." Everyone breathed easier. "We were afraid his heart had been ruptured and that he was bleeding internally. We don't think that is the case now, but we want to keep him overnight . . . ." The doctor talked on, but Judy was no longer listening. She was deeply thankful that her son's life was spared, and that her grandchildren still had their father.

But many grandparents have found ways to be successful at helping an extended family through a severe crisis. The loss of a parent or child may render some family members incapable of functioning for a time. Families dealing with death need time to weep, to grieve.

Grandparents can be a vital resource during these times of sorrow and adjustment if they will follow three guidelines.

Guideline #1: Be there. The very presence of a loving grandparent is reassuring to a child who has to deal with the fact that Daddy is not going to come home from the hospital. The sense of well-being that comes from Grandma and Grandpa's steady presence cannot be overestimated. When some teenagers were asked what they most wanted from their grandparents during a crisis, they replied, "Being there." Why? Because it signified to them that they would get through; that life would stabilize again.

Life is difficult. It's painful. Sometimes the hurt seems more than we can bear. The very presence of Grandma and Grandpa is a solid source of comfort and help. We provide warm, accepting, understanding shoulders to cry on. We can help with common chores that seem overwhelming under the burden of grief. We can drive the children to school. We can make lunch or take care of dinner. We can gently help with the funeral arrangements, lending a wisdom and experience gained over the years. Most of all, we can provide a sense of faith, security, and connectedness. "Grandma, Dad is in heaven. Mom is crying most of the time. I don't know what is going to happen. It makes me feel secure to know that you and Grandpa are here."

Guideline #2: Be a source of faith. When families are running short of trust in God, grandparents can express and model their faith in God. It's difficult to feel that a loving God is in control when you've watched your little girl die slowly in a hospital after only three weeks of life. It's unbelievably tough for children to understand how God could let their mom or dad or sibling die. It usually isn't much help when a well-meaning friend quotes Scripture and talks about God's providence. But the tragedy is easier to accept when Grandma tearfully tells you that her third child died of polio. As she expresses the pain that was part of that loss, telling you how the presence and power of God carried her through, she brings you comfort and hope. It's reassuring to see Grandpa on his knees every morning and overhear him speak to God on behalf of his family.

Faith in God is vital and reassuring during a tragedy. Those who have it see their way through the struggles; those who don't find more difficulty in moving on with their lives. As grandparents, our living, vital relationship with Jesus can be an inspiration to the whole family.

> Blessed be the God and Father of our Lord Jesus Christ, the Father of mercies and God of all comfort, who comforts us in all our tribulation, that we may be able to comfort those who are in any trouble, with the comfort with which we ourselves are comforted by God. For as the sufferings of Christ abound in us, so our consolation also abounds through Christ. (2 Cor. 1:3-5)

On the basis of this verse, most grandparents have earned the right to speak of God's comfort during a tragedy. Their faith has carried them through many rough places and difficult times. They have been taught by the years, not only by sermons and books. Grandparents who have learned the hard-taught lessons of faith must share what they have learned with their grieving, questioning families.

Guideline #3: Express your own grief. If your grandchild is being buried, please don't feel that you have to keep up a strong facade "so you don't upset the children." Your grief is real, and you must take your place as mourner. It's not your job to bear all the family burdens at the expense of your own emotional and spiritual health. Give yourself the freedom to express your grief. Let the loss show. It's important for your children and grandchildren to see your grief. Feeling a deep sense of sadness and loss following the death of a loved one is natural; it is not a sign of weak faith. Let your grandchildren see you grieve, but not as those "who have no hope" (1 Thess. 4:13). Because you are sorrowing, you let them know that it's okay for them to cry too. That in turn will make the adjustment to the loss easier for everyone.

Grandparenting a disabled child

"Mom! Dad! It's a boy! But something's wrong. The doctors will be doing more tests, but they think Todd is a Down's syndrome baby."

Bill and Karen were delighted at the birth of their grandson, but this was not the kind of news they had waited for hours to hear. Their third grandchild, the first boy, had Down's syndrome. The words had a somber ring. They had sometimes looked aside when mothers walked by in the mall with their Down's children, never dreaming they would have to deal with a disability in their own family. Grandparenting had always been easy before, but now a test had come. Bill and Karen wondered, Will we love this child as much? Will our daughter-in-law have to quit her job to take care of Todd full time? If so, how will they cope financially? What does this news mean to the family?

Parents of developmentally disabled children were asked in a survey how others, especially grandparents, best helped them as they reared their handicapped children in a sometimes unaccommodating world. The first source of help came in what can be categorized as *functional* areas. Parents listed support in practical ways such as providing a ride to the doctor and helping with household chores. These parents expressed gratitude for grandparents who were willing to babysit, providing them a brief respite from the responsibilities. Grandparents were also helpful during medical emergencies, especially when there were other children in the family. These are practical helps that creative grandparents of "differently abled" children can readily provide.

The second aspect of assistance was *emotional*. Parents were pleased when their moms and dads made an effort to understand the special needs and struggles of handicapped children. They also emphasized that grandparents who understood the pressure the handicap put on the unity of the entire family were of special encouragement and help. Letting the parents express their feelings freely, without judging them, was invaluable.

Most of all, creative grandparents of a handicapped child can offer an *empathetic relationship* with the child's parents. It can sometimes be a heavy burden to parent a disabled child. Parents often feel that they must carry it alone. Creative grandparents find acceptable ways to put their shoulders under the burden too, so they can help carry the weight.

Grandparenting during death, family trauma, or disability is sometimes very hard. It calls on us to open ourselves to pain and suffering, to carry part of the load, to bear one another's burdens (Gal. 6:2). To be honest, Judy and I have not been called on to experience much of this firsthand. We have been spared the stress of divorce, death, or disability. Yet we have admired grandparents who have come through these trials with flying colors. We have observed grandparents whose pride in their "differently abled" grandchildren has burst out of them for all to see. As a counselor, I have seen grandparents become the glue that held the family together during a severe crisis such as a serious accident, death, or divorce.

Creative grandparents are willing to deal with life head-on. They accept its twists and turns, its wide-open pathways and sudden dead-ends. We know and accept that life is difficult. We have learned that being alive means bearing pain. But we also know that life's greatest joys come through its deepest trials. And we remember the promises of the One who said He would never leave us or forsake us, the One who referred to Himself as "the God of all comfort," and the One who commanded us to bear one another's burdens with grace.

Chapter Five

Long-Distance Grandparenting

Ken and Joyce welcomed their first grandchild into the world with high expectations. Joyce had recently spent a week with her daughter Dianne, helping her prepare her home for the arrival of the little one. The parents called her Katie, and her birth brought her grandparents great joy.

Ken and Joyce were deeply involved in Katie's life right from the beginning, and they planned to be her life-long friends. They eagerly anticipated experiencing the world again through her beautiful blue eyes, and it was happening. Joyce especially took to this little girl, and she felt her love was returned tenfold by Katie. Life was just about perfect for Ken and Joyce. Katie lived only about thirty minutes away, and they saw her often. They felt sure it would always be that way.

At least that was their dream.

Ken was a successful and beloved pastor. He had urged his congregation many times to give their children to God. He had even pounded the pulpit for emphasis as he said, "Don't hold back your children from the Lord's service. Our prayer should be that our children will grow up wanting to serve God." He and Joyce sincerely believed what he was saying. But then it was their turn.

They learned that Jim, Dianne, and Katie were moving. Not just to a nearby town; not even to a faraway state. Katie's parents had responded to the call of God to become missionaries. They were moving to Uruguay. That's in South America!

Ken and Joyce watched sadly as their daughter, son-in-law, and granddaughter boarded the plane that would take them first to Miami, then to Montevideo. They faced a future that did not have little Katie nearby to light up their lives with her flashing smile and loving hugs. As they drove slowly home, the questions began to come. How were they going to stay a part of Katie's life? Since she was only two, would she recognize them when she returned after four years? How could they be a positive influence on her life when she was thousands of miles away?

Grandparenting from a distance is increasingly common in today's world. Although most will not have to deal with the distance or duration Ken and Joyce did, many grandparents are forced to cope with the reality of long miles between them and the grandchildren they love.

Sometimes grandparents retire, move to warmer southern and western climes, and go to enjoy life. They are also choosing to say good-bye to their grandchildren. Divorce may mean relocation for the custodial parent, sometimes far from Grandma and Grandpa. The increasing mobility of our culture contributes to the rise of long-range grandparenting. Parents change jobs, are transferred, and relocate more now than ever. Gone are the days of growing up, attending school, and working all your life in the same town your father did. These factors all contribute to the growing number of grandparents who must find ways to fulfill their important role from a distance.

Grandparenting is a time-intensive activity. The major prerequisite to being involved in the lives of your grandchildren is being there. If we do not see them regularly, we feel that we cannot be a major part of their lives. And distance often determines how frequently we see them. Grandparents who live within ten miles of their grandchildren average forty visits per year with them, while those who live more than one hundred miles away average only three visits a year. Distance is the single most important factor influencing the amount of time grandparents spend with their grandchildren. Long-distance grandparents are at a severe disadvantage!

If you live far from your grandchildren, you may be asking the same questions Ken and Joyce were. How can we be a factor in the lives of our grandchildren when so many miles separate us?

In this chapter we will look first, and without flinching, at the pain of grandparenting from a distance. Then we will analyze the problems associated with long-distance grandparenting. We will examine the possibilities for long-distance grandparents who want to be involved in the lives of their faraway grandchildren. Finally, we will talk about the preparation required to make visits with them enjoyable and productive.

The pain of long-distance grandparenting

As Joyce talked about Katie, her eyes filled with tears and her voice was hoarse with emotion. Saying good-bye was painful and difficult. She had enjoyed grandmothering Katie, and they had bonded deeply. It hurt to see her leave. Yet every long-distance grandmother goes for lengthy periods of time without seeing her grandchildren. Every one of those grandparents hurts with each separation. We must face it. Pain is part of long-distance grandparenting.

Grandparents who see their little loved ones infrequently speak of missing the little things that make up their personalities.

"I miss the way he says his s's when he says, 'Pleathe push me in the thwing again, Grandpa.'"

"I really miss having her crawl into bed with me during a thunderstorm. She doesn't make a big deal of it. She just slips quietly down the hall and into Grandma's room. Then she reaches over for my hand, squeezes it, and goes back to sleep."

"I miss him bringing his girlfriends over to my house so I can get to meet them. 'I just don't want to date someone you don't like, Grandma.' That's what he always tells me."

"I miss the big hugs and kisses."

"I miss roasting hot dogs in the fireplace. Then messy marshmallows, burned to a crisp."

"I missed seeing him take his first steps and ride his bike the first time without training wheels. I wish I could have been there for that."

Each of these grandparents is expressing the same sentiment. They miss being with their grandchildren, and it brings them pain. They get notes like this:

> *Dear Grandma,*
> *Thank you for the birthday present. But I miss you. I wish you were here. Come and visit us soon. It's snowing a lot. I got nice presents.*
> *Love, Molly*

Pain is part of long-distance grandparenting. But pain is just one of the problems. Grandparents with many miles between them and their grandchildren must also find answers to these difficult questions:

- How can I be a positive influence?
- How can I get to know my grandchildren when I seldom see them?
- Will they get to know me? Will they remember me?
- What can I expect from my grandchildren when I do see them?

These are real questions without easy answers. The truth is that it is more difficult to grandparent from a distance than when the children are close. But it is not impossible. You can be a creative, involved grandparent, even though half a continent separates you from those grandchildren you love. It takes careful thought, lots of planning, some creativity, and a willingness to accept the challenge. But you can do it. So get your creative juices flowing and observe how some other grandparents are succeeding at being long-distance grandparents.

Ways to be a positive influence

Ken and Joyce made a playroom in their house that was Katie's exclusive domain. They haven't changed it since she left. They wonder how their two-year-old granddaughter will be able to remember her favorite places at Grandma's house when she probably won't be there again until she is six years old. One solution is through modern technology. They are making a videotape of the places Katie enjoyed. On the tape is the swing set in the park, the room she slept in when she visited Grandma and Grandpa, and her own playroom—complete with stove, table and chairs, and tea set. As Katie grows older, the video tape will be a conversation starter for her parents as they tell Katie about Grandma and Grandpa. It will serve as a visual reminder that even though they are far away, her grandparents still love her and are thinking about her.

Video cameras seem to have been invented for long-distance grandparents. Try to get your hands on one for at least a couple days every year. They are an invaluable tool for keeping in touch with your grandchildren.

One grandparent wanted to teach his Christian values to his teenage grandson. So he rented a video camera and narrated the tale of his youthful adventures. He had footage of the exact places his mistakes were made. He videotaped the sharp curve in the road where he had crashed his car when driving while drinking. He told his grandson how he had nearly died.

He went to the junk yard to see if the first car he ever owned was still there, because in that car he had stolen his first kiss. As he told the story, he gave some clear warnings about relating with girls. He narrated many of the experiences of his life on the tape, passing along the lessons he learned and the values he had grown to accept.

When the package with the tape arrived, his grandson was at first disappointed. (No money was in the package.) He let the video sit unwatched for several days. Then one evening his parents returned home to find him sprawled in front of the TV, watching as Grandpa narrated his life story. This apparently nonchalant teen was enthralled by the tales of his grandfather's youth. Grandpa had succeeded in teaching his grandson about life and his faith in God through the use of technology.

Grandparents could also help grandchildren visualize what an impending visit with Grandma and Grandpa

would be like. They could videotape some of the fun places they might go and things they might do. There could
be scenes from the malls, the zoo, the beach, the back-
yard, or the park. Viewing the tape would excite the children about visiting Grandma and Grandpa.

The uses creative grandparents could make of a video camera are limited only by their imagination—and
their patience with learning how to run the thing.

The telephone is another way for creative grandparents to be a positive influence on their faraway grandchildren. It can really be "the next best thing to being there,"
especially when used with a little imagination.

If Grandpa and Grandson share a common love for
baseball, for example, they could actually watch the
World Series together on the phone. Sure, it costs money—but it's cheaper than a plane ticket! It's simple to
turn on the TV and call your grandson after key plays,
applauding or criticizing the players, and berating the
umpires for their obvious vision defects.

The same could be done in watching your favorite
TV shows together. Or for special programs you and your
granddaughter are both interested in.

The phone can also be a way to spend regularly
scheduled time with your granddaughter or grandson.
Grandmother, for example, can have a regularly scheduled Saturday morning or Sunday afternoon phone date
with her granddaughter. It's a time when they share the
week, and they can enjoy the sound of each other's voice.
All it takes is the desire to make it a priority. And the approval of Mom and Dad.

Some truly high-tech grandparents even connect
with their teenage grandchildren through their personal
computers. These machines are equipped with a modem

that allows communication over the phone lines. Hip grandparents can send messages to their grandchild's computer. They can even send pictures and drawings back and forth between the computers. Imagine the reaction of a teenager writing a report on his computer (a gift from Grandma). He takes a minute to check his computer mail for messages, and there's a letter from Grandma telling about her trip to the Grand Canyon—complete with pictures of her astride a horse on the South Rim. Once again, a little desire and imagination makes excellent communication possible.

If you are not into technology, how about writing every week? As often as possible, enclose a photo of you doing something lively and interesting. The letter does not have to be as literary as Hemingway reporting on the running of the bulls. "Hi! How are you doing? I think about you a lot and I wondered how you were getting along. This is me playing golf." That kind of note will do the job.

Letter-writing is a great way for some of us who have difficulty verbalizing our feelings to tell our grandchildren what they mean to us. What we may not be able to say to their faces, we can put into words on paper and send off. All grandchildren, no matter what age, like to hear that Grandma or Grandpa thinks they're great.

To make it even more special, you might want to purchase matching stationery for you and each grandchild. Explain to them that this stationery is to be used only when you write one another. Imagine the excitement when the special envelope comes! It means a letter from Grandma! Or from Granddaughter! Specialness always makes children (and grandparents) feel loved and unique.

The mail is also a way to share common interests, or to exchange information about important events. The grandson who sends Grandma a picture of his little sister, as well as a running commentary on his latest Little League exploits, will warm her heart. Likewise, grandparents can send baseball cards to their collecting grandson or granddaughter. Or they can send press clippings or magazine articles about their grandchild's favorite athletes, television stars, or music personalities.

A brave grandfather may even listen to the music his granddaughters like. He could even send them tickets to a concert in their area. He passes along his grousings about the lyrics and beat, of course. But they love Grandpa's reviews of the latest from U2 or Garth Brooks.

Once again, the limit to your involvement with grandchildren who live far away is determined more by the intensity of your desire to be their friend and a creative, involved grandparent than it is by the miles that separate you. Some grandparents who live on the same block as their grandchildren are not involved in their lives. It's a matter of choice and priority. The question is this: How much do we want to make a difference in the lives of our distant grandchildren? Do we care enough to watch a game with them on the phone? Do we want to stay in touch enough to write regularly? Will we go to the trouble and expense to purchase or rent a video camera? I hope so!

We can be a positive influence on our grandchildren from miles away. It takes energy and ingenuity, but we can do it!

Getting to know you

Using the methods introduced above, we can get to know our long-distance grandchildren and let them get to know us. If you choose letter-writing, you might try the following:

• Initiate a writing project. Challenge the grandchildren to write about their activities, friends, school, and feelings.

• Provide the grandchildren with a written history of the family. Use one of those books with blank pages, and fill it in with important dates, events, descriptions, and memories. Include pictures and sketches.

• Write about interesting events from your childhood, teenage years, college days, or military experience. Pass along your good childhood memories. Tell the funny stuff.

• Include some of the hard times: long months without a job, empty cupboards during the Depression, Grandma's slow recovery from an illness. Describe what happened when Thad broke his leg. Create a sense of family strength and courage.

• Have the grandchildren describe a typical school day or tell you what they do on Sunday.

• The younger children can always draw a picture of something they enjoyed doing or somewhere they went.

• Describe for the grandchildren a fun experience or trip you enjoyed. Be sure to talk about feelings.

• Include a lot of humor. Show them that life can be fun even when it's serious and difficult.

These are ways of letting your grandchildren into your life by letter, and of getting into theirs. You'll soon discover you don't feel like strangers when you are able to get together. You'll already have plenty to talk about.

Never overlook your camera as a means of enhancing your relationship with your faraway grandchildren. You will communicate volumes about yourself and your life through pictures. Grandmother Nancy, who lives in New Jersey, regularly sends photographs as postcards to her Michigan grandchildren. She draws a line down the middle of the back of the picture, puts the name, address, and stamp on the proper side, jots a short note explaining the photo, and drops it in the mail. This helps her grandchildren keep her face fresh in their minds. They know what her interests are, and they have a pretty clear idea of what her home and her part of the country is like. And these "picture postcards" always end up on the refrigerator door, or on the bulletin boards in the child's room.

Your grandchildren need to know that you do more than sit in a rocking chair and knit sweaters. Explain through letters, audio tapes, and videos what your life consists of. Let your grandchildren get a feel for your eccentric friends—and your own humorous quirks as well. Yes, you can let them deep into your life even though you are not nearby.

George and Judy were missionaries to Taiwan. They were not in the U.S. for the births of their daughter's first two children. They knew that the cost of travel would prohibit frequent visits home. Understanding that it would confuse the children to have two people called Grandma and Grandpa. Especially if they had never seen one set of them, they came up with a plan. They would be known as Grammie and Gramps, as opposed to Grandma and Grandpa. It worked out well. Erin and Jonathan understood from an early age that far across the ocean lived two people who cared for them very much called Grammie and Gramps. They were Mom's parents, and they loved them just as much as Grandma and Grandpa did.

A great-grandmother lived in Montana. Because of poor health and economic factors, she never got to see her faraway grandchildren. But they knew her as Momma Montana. They heard from her frequently, and they knew that she loved them. Her picture went up on the bulletin boards in their rooms, along with other family photos. They prayed for her, along with the rest of the family.

It would be simple to sit in our easy chairs and complain about the miles that keep us from getting to know our grandchildren. How much better to get up out of that chair and do something about it! Arthur Kornhaber, a researcher and grandparent himself, wrote, "Too many grandparents, when they retire, are dropping out of family life and abandoning their grandchildren. Instead of running off to the Sun Belt to play shuffleboard in the sun, their goal as grandparents should be to nurture the younger generations, and to play an active role as emotional leaders of the extended family." This can be done from a distance, if we are willing to stretch our imaginations and drop some of our inhibitions.

Preparing for visits

A final ingredient of long-range grandparenting is preparation for visits. To make the most of the short time long-distance grandparents and their grandchildren have together, be sure to prepare for visits in advance. This is important whether we go to see our grandchildren or they come to visit us.

It's a treat to have our grandchildren all to ourselves. There is something special about being their only companions for a few days. We enjoy seeing them outside their usual environment and having them in our world.

Often, however, the anticipation is more fun than the actual visit because we have not prepared properly. We feel relieved when they leave, yet we also feel guilty because we didn't do all we could have with them. Careful forethought and simple planning can go a long way toward ensuring that the next visit is more satisfying.

We must first answer some basic questions. Are our grandchildren old enough to come "all by themselves" for a visit? How often should they come? Should we offer to pay all the expenses, including travel? What will we do with them while they are here?

In his book *How To Grandparent*, Fitzhugh Dodson recommends that children be at least five years old before they visit on their own. Most airlines permit children of this age to travel alone on an airplane. You may fret a little at the idea of a five-year-old traveling solo, but the airlines do a wonderful job of taking care of their little passengers. They assist them with boarding and de-planing, and they give them special attention and companionship during a layover or change of planes. As long as you are there on time to meet them, they should not experience any difficulty at all.

Your young grandchild will almost certainly experience some homesickness on the visit. But that is not crippling and usually can be dealt with by wise parental preparation and understanding grandparents. Bringing along a much-loved doll or stuffed animal will help. So will a reminder of how many days before they see Mom and Dad again. A phone call home may become necessary, but try to save it as a last resort.

Before you suggest a visit to the child, be sure to talk it over with her parents and get their okay. Discuss the logistics of travel and time before extending the invitation to the child. Nothing is more aggravating to a parent than to have to be the bad guy and say no to a child because Grandpa went ahead and scheduled a visit without clearing it with Mom and Dad first.

As for the length of the visit, it is important to know your grandchild. You also need to have something for your grandchild to do at your house. If you live in Orlando, a visit of two weeks might not be long enough to do everything. Certainly Orlando offers plenty for any age grandchild to do. On the other hand, if you live on a remote island off the coast of Maine and your grandchildren are city dwellers, two weeks could seem like an eternity. Keep this principle in mind: Try to arrange for your grandchild to leave wishing he could have stayed longer rather than waiting sullenly for his departure date. As a general rule, start with a visit of just a few days. As your grandchildren grow and mature, adjust the length of the visits appropriately.

How often should grandchildren visit? When should they visit? The answers to these questions depends on you and their parents. How much free time do you have? Will you be taking vacation time to be with them? Or are you retired? How much energy do you have? Do you have the means to fly your grandchildren to your home more than once a year? Or is every other year your limit? Only you can answer these questions. Perhaps the parents could cover the cost of one visit and you the next. Once again, your individual situation will determine the frequency and length of the visits. Even a family of modest means can scrimp for a visit to Grandma—watching for special airfares—when it's made a priority.

Summer vacation is usually a great time for most school-age grandchildren to visit Grandma and Grandpa.

Around the middle of July, mothers and fathers will appreciate a break from their active, vacationing children. By then the children are growing bored with doing the same old things. A visit with Grandma and Grandpa may be just the change everyone would welcome.

If grandparents live in the Sun Belt, and their grandchildren reside in the frozen Midwest or Northeast, Christmas break is a good time for a visit. Do not interfere with the family's Christmas celebration by unexpectedly proposing that the grandchildren spend the holiday with you. Most parents would rather spend Christmas with all their family together—and they should! You might propose flying the children out just after Christmas and have them return after New Year's Day. Remember, always schedule the trip with the parents before discussing it with your grandchildren.

You might talk about two or three possible dates for a visit, including spring break, and letting the children themselves decide. This gives the grandchildren some feeling of control. It will also keep them from feeling that they've been "shipped off" and gotten out of Mom and Dad's hair.

The most important question facing grandparents when their grandchildren visit is this: What will we do with them once they get here? After we have hugged and kissed at the airport, stopped at their favorite fast-food restaurant on the way home, and unpacked, what do we do? Here are four principles to follow when planning activities for your visiting grandchildren, whether they are five or fifteen years of age.

Be available. The first and most important key to a happy, satisfying visit is to loosen up that schedule of yours. I know grandparents who look forward all year to a visit from their grandchildren, then refuse to cancel a golf match or pass up their regular Thursday brunch with the girls. You need to maximize your availability while the grandchildren are there. If you are not yet retired, take some time off. Find a substitute for the golf or summer bowling league. Grandchildren—especially the younger ones—will be disappointed if they have to play second-fiddle to Grandma or Grandpa's packed schedule.

Our bingo games or women's clubs are not nearly as important as our grandchildren! For that matter, neither are business meetings or board meetings. The broker can wait. As long-distance grandparents, your time with these precious children is already restricted. When they are able to come, let them know how important they are and how much you love them by taking the trouble to re-schedule your lives around them. Even the youngest grandchildren will realize what you've done, and it will communicate your love very clearly.

When you talk to the parents after a visit, never make a big deal about what you had to give up to spend time with your grandchildren. Their response may be, "If it's such a big sacrifice, Dad, forget it. It's really easier for us to keep them at home anyway. You don't have to worry about putting yourself out again, because you won't be given the opportunity." Creative grandparents are willing to give their time to their grandchildren, to watch them grow, to find joy in their presence. Be available!

Be flexible. Flexibility is also a vital factor in making your grandchild's visit a success. We often look forward so eagerly to these rare opportunities that we create rigid, unrealistic expectations of what the week will be like.

We expect our grandchildren to leap into our arms immediately and love us completely and without reservation. That's not the way it usually works. Younger grandchildren may take a couple of days to warm up to a grandma and grandpa they haven't seen for many weeks or months. Older grandchildren may be embarrassed by your affection. They may wonder if you will like the changes they have undergone since you last saw them. Don't put enormous pressure on them, or yourself, to keep things the same. And don't expect the week to be one enormous success after another (by your definition). Don't try to relive past moments of glory every year.

One grandmother treasured the yearly visits of her two young grandchildren. She lived on an old farm and they lived in the city. Every year they visited, they worked together in the garden and the children loved it. They would go to the woods and fields behind the house and pick wild strawberries and blueberries. It was a tradition Grandma and grandchildren looked forward to. They would pick fresh fruit and Grandma would make it into a pie for dinner. But when the oldest granddaughter, Tina, turned thirteen, she didn't want to pick berries anymore. She was more interested in the boys who lived on the farm down the road. Grandma was hurt and angry. What was wrong with Tina? Didn't she love Grandma anymore? Why couldn't she just do what she always did? Was she just trying to be difficult?

The answer to these questions, of course, is no. Tina was growing up. Her needs and interests had changed as her body had changed. Grandma made the mistake of assuming her thirteen-year-old granddaughter was the same as the seven-year-old who had eaten more wild strawberries than she had put in the bucket. The girl had changed, and Grandma's expectations needed to change as well.

One sure way to wreck a visit with your grandchildren is to weigh it down with expectations. Be flexible. Realize that a year or even six months can make a tremendous difference in your grandchild. It might be a good idea not to schedule the first few days too full of activities they loved on the previous visit. Use that time to get to know the children again, determine where they are, and discover what they like to do. Find a place that's comfortable for both of you and build on it.

Establish traditions. Being flexible does not preclude the establishment of family traditions. Large and small traditions provide continuity for grandparents and grandchildren who see each other infrequently. They can provide a starting point for the renewal of a dormant relationship. When these traditions are not laden with weighty expectations, they can provide a safe and familiar means of remembering and renewing the relationship.

We lived a considerable distance from my parents when our children were small. Sometimes the infrequency of the visits made our first few hours together somewhat awkward. Jon had a solution for this. His grandma always baked yellow cupcakes with vanilla frosting when she knew the boys were coming. When we arrived, Jon never even tried to enter into small talk with his grandparents. He went right to the kitchen of the rambling old farmhouse in search of Grandma's cupcakes. His first words were invariably the same. "Grandma, where are the cupcakes? I've been thinking about them the whole trip." What started as a simple, one-time event became a tradition that eased grandparents and grand-children into a warm relationship.

The tradition continued fifteen years. On each trip to Grandma's, Jon and Jack would talk about having a cupcake before doing anything else. Grandma loved it. Jon is now in his late twenties, with two children of his own. But he still goes into the kitchen every time he visits Grandma to see if there are cupcakes. And more often than not, there are.

This is a simple little tradition. Others carry much more significance.

Grandma couldn't wait for Lisa, her ten-year-old granddaughter, to arrive for her visit. You see, Lisa had turned ten, and that was a special age for the girls in Grandma's family. Grandma began teaching the girls to sew when they became ten. Beginning with her first granddaughter nearly fifteen years earlier, she had decided that she would instruct each granddaughter in this skill that she had learned over a lifetime. What began as a desire to pass on something of lifelong use became a tradition. When each granddaughter reached age ten, she spent a week with Grandma during the summer learning to sew. Younger girls always asked, "Can I do it now?" But grandmother knew the virtue in patience and the importance of fairness, so each granddaughter had to wait her turn.

When their tenth birthday finally came and summer vacation began, the girl would receive a formal invitation from Grandma. "Dear Lisa: I would very much like for you to visit me this summer for one week. You are now ten years old, and it would be my pleasure to begin to teach you how to sew." The letter went on, but those somewhat formal words were music to the ears of that girl. As for Grandma, well, she started teaching them to sew because she thought it was important for them to know how. The skill was valuable to her, and she wanted to pass it along.

As Grandma grew older, the girls seemed to get younger. Every year it became more difficult to find things to talk about. But there was always the sewing. Some girls became quite adept with the needle and thread and machine. Others never got the hang of it. It didn't matter to Grandma. She treasured the hours they spent together—hours spent over patterns, looking at her granddaughter's beautiful profile, and the way she cocked her head when she really concentrated.

Grandma was hesitant to talk about music or boys when her granddaughters reached their teenage years, but she could usually start a vigorous conversation with, "I remember when you were ten and it was the first time you put a piece of cloth through a sewing machine . . . ." Her granddaughter's face would soften, and the years that separated them would disappear—along with their differences in values and preoccupations. That tradition was a source of strength in their relationship.

Traditions are extremely important in long-distance grandparenting. They provide a point of contact for grandparents and grandchildren. They become a way to remember Grandpa. It is difficult to remember him abstractly, but the memories of the fishing trips, or the daily walks to the store for a newspaper (and a candy bar), or the bowling outing the first night at his house is easy. Traditions make the miles wear less on the memory.

To lessen the distance between you and your faraway grandchildren, establish traditions. Beware, however, of forcing them on your grandchildren. They need to be fun for everyone involved. Look carefully at the things you now do with your grandchildren. You probably already have traditions in the making. Point them out to your grandchildren. Let them know that you value those traditions as much as they do, that you respect their involvement in them, and that you want them to continue. But if they do outgrow them, let the traditions die.

Traditions become important sources of shared memories and laughter later on. As our precious little grandchildren turn into adults, the warmth we receive from remembering long-standing traditions cannot be overstated. We'll think about them often. And we'll draw often on the common ground they established as the years go by.

Let them lead. A final principle for long-distance visits with grandchildren is to let the children lead. As advised earlier with wonder-years grandchildren, try to follow the child's agenda. During the visit, follow their interests and desires. You have fifty-one weeks of the year to "do your own thing." When they arrive, let them set the activities. Let them tell you what they want to do and how they would like to spend their time. Offer them a variety of choices. Listen to their suggestions.

Some grandparents give their visiting grandchildren a choice between going bowling at the Starlight Lanes or the Idle Hour Alleys. In reality, that is not a choice at all. A real choice would be between bowling, miniature golf, going to the beach, or shopping at the mall. Let your grandchildren help you decide—then do it!

Letting them lead means that we are making them the most important people in our lives while they are with us. We say they are the center of our lives, but we are often quite determined to do what we want during visits. Be aware of that temptation and fight it. Giving children a voice in decisions demonstrates our love for them and reinforces their worth.

When you visit them

It's a little different when you go to your grandchildren's home. A successful visit requires you to use tact, discretion, and unselfishness. The keys to visiting your grandchildren on their turf are really quite simple:

- Realize where you are.
- Share your grandchildren.
- Be quiet.
- Be adaptable.

Realize where you are. When we arrive from out of town for the purpose of visiting our children and grandchildren, we must remember that we are the guests. Our children have busy lives that do not revolve around us. Even though they may be thrilled to see us, they may also see us as somewhat of a pain. The first key to having a successful visit, then, is to realize, in Dorothy's words to Toto, "We're not in Kansas anymore." We are not in our environment. We don't make the rules here. Our children do. Our job is to abide by the bedtime wishes they have for their children, by their feelings about candy, by their approach to discipline, and everything else. Realize where you are.

Learn to share your grandchildren. True, we're the visitors— the guests. But we still have to share those precious children with school, their friends, their parents, and their own interests and activities.

When they visit us, we are usually the focal point of their interest. They are in a strange city. They don't know anyone. By nature they cling to us and make us the center of their universe. But when we visit them, it's different. Their everyday activities and friendships keep on going. We are just one of their interests. For example, when they visit us, our teenage grandchildren may enjoy our hugs and kisses. But in front of their parents and siblings, they may be embarrassed and pull away. That's okay. It doesn't mean they don't love you. It means we are on their turf, and we have to be sensitive to their feelings and the forces that are pulling them in so many different directions. We have to share them, so we might as well get used to it.

Be quiet. You may not like the way your children do the disciplining. Whether they are too strict or too lenient, chances are it won't be to your liking. Stifle the impulse to comment on everything you find wrong. Don't speak to your children about it as if they were eleven years old again. So, the third rule for a successful visit is this: be quiet. We haven't been invited to critique our children's parenting skills or to grade them on their housekeeping. We are there as loving grandparents.

What can be more dangerous than a grandmother who has always been a combination of Mr. Clean and the Tidy Bowl Man? Dust is her enemy, and dirt is anathema. Her son marries a nice girl who is an average housekeeper. Grandma visits, can't stand it, and decides to set new standards for her daughter-in-law. (She may even be secretly concerned about the health of her grandchildren.) So she starts to make remarks and give suggestions. How do you suppose that daughter-in-law feels?

Like a miserable failure; that Grandma doesn't think she's good enough for her son or grandchildren.

One family handled criticism this way. The son came to his mother and said directly, "Mom, if you can't accept the way we live, go back home. I know you love the grandchildren, and we all love you, but there will be no more visits like this one." Grandma sputtered. She cried. But she realized that the house was basically clean, and she accepted the fact that her son was right. She had violated one of the basic rules of visiting grandchildren: be quiet. Now she keeps her thoughts to herself, and the visits continue.

Be adaptable. This principle for trouble-free visits to our grandchildren goes beyond being flexible. To be adaptable means not only putting aside your daily rituals and plans, but accepting the rituals and schedule of the household you are visiting. Make the effort to fit right in. Your ability to adapt to their routine and lifestyle will make the visit far less stressful and far more pleasant.

Long-distance grandparenting can be a painful, problem-filled experience. But with a little planning and creativity, it can also be relatively trouble-free and satisfying. It's up to us. We can let the miles defeat us and turn us into spectators as our grandchildren grow into young men and women. Or we can put ourselves into the starting lineup and play a major league role in their development. Our challenge to you is this: Make the effort to be involved, creative grandparents. The miles are a hindrance, requiring creativity and ingenuity on your part. But they don't need to stop you from being an important part of your grandchildren's lives.

Checklist for creative grandparents

❑ I have accepted the fact that my grandchildren live far away.

❑ I have stopped complaining about it.

❑ I have determined to communicate weekly or monthly with each of my faraway grandchildren.

❑ I know which works best for me: letters or phone calls.

❑ I have sent them a picture of me in my world in the last three months.

❑ I send packages on birthdays, Christmas, and special occasions.

❑ I have established some traditions with my distant grandchildren.

❑ I visit them at least once a year.

❑ They visit me when their parents feel they are old enough.

❑ I have done some reading about middle-years and teenage grandchildren so I know what to expect and how best to relate to them.

❑ I have investigated how I can help them with their education.

❑ I make it a practice to clear each suggestion with their parents.

Chapter Six

You and Your Children

"I wish I could have started as a grandparent. You know, just sort of skipped over the whole parenting bit and be- gun by being a grandpa immediately. I guess the fact that you have to be a parent before you can be a grandparent proves that God has a sense of humor."

As we interviewed grandparents for this book, we heard comments like this again and again. That's because so many of us struggled as parents. Our children didn't turn out quite as we had hoped. Along the way they made detours that scared the daylights out of us. Our an- ger at what we perceived as our own children's failings shamed us, and our shame made us even more angry. We doubted our parenting skills. "Am I doing it right? Is there a right way at all? How come children don't come with a set of instructions as toys do?"

No doubt about it: Parenting can be a tough job— one that few first-time parents are really prepared for. We had to learn as we went. As parents we had to "take our medicine," and most of the time it tasted like castor oil. By contrast, grandparenting is like a slice of chocolate chip cheesecake—pretty easy to take!

The joy we derive from grandparenting can cause us to ignore our children—the foundation for our relation- ship with our grandchildren. We must realize that our re- lationship with our adult children directly and profoundly influences our relationship with our beloved grandchildren. We can't pretend that nothing came before. Our past, lived in full view of our children, plays a large role in our grandparenting.

To grandparent effectively and creatively, therefore, we must have healthy, strong relationships with our children. Let's illustrate. Jim loves being a grandparent. He can't wait to be with his grandsons, ages seven, five, and three. Some might even say that he spoils those boys when they come to visit. If you suggested that to him, however, he would defend himself by pointing out that he gets them only four times a year.

But Jim is not a long-distance grandparent. His grandsons only live about twenty-five minutes away. But Jim and his daughter do not get along. She thought he was a lousy parent, and he thought she was an ungrateful kid. The bitterness between them grew after she moved out. They have not resolved the hurt and anger of the past. Jim sees his grandchildren only four times a year because that's all his daughter allows. He is miserable because he is not a bigger part of their lives. His poor relationship with his daughter diminishes his time and connection with his grandsons.

In this chapter we will examine the parent-child relationship as it affects grandparenting. We will look first at the importance of maintaining a healthy relationship with our adult children. Next, we will analyze the changing dynamics of our relationship with our adult children. Finally, we will suggest ways to reconcile relationships that are burdened with unresolved conflict.

Grandparenting, especially the involved, creative grandparenting we've been advocating, is impossible without the support of your children. But you may be at odds with them. If so, this may be the most important chapter for you. As we begin, you need to realize that rediscovering your children can be a painful process. But it can bring cleansing and healing. Take a deep breath, then, and get ready for a long look back as we discuss creative grandparenting as it relates to you and your children.

The importance of a good relationship
We cannot overstate the effect your relationship with your children has on your grandparenting. In fact, your satisfaction as a grandparent depends on it. Two words sum up the reason for this: *access* and *attitude*.

Access. Our children control our access to our grandchildren. We may envision them as the conduit to our grandchildren. If they choose not to let us see them, or if they restrict the amount of time we can spend with them, our lives will be less fulfilling.

It doesn't take a nuclear physicist to figure out that creative grandparenting depends on access. Long-distance grandparents have to rely on their children for access through cards and phone calls. And when we live nearby, our children control the day-by-day events of our grandchildren's lives.

To illustrate the importance of access, let's look at Alice and Mary. Neighbors in a small town, each has a five-year-old grandson. Alice's grandson lives about thirty miles from her home. Mary's lives more than two-hundred miles away, in a suburb of Chicago. Last summer Mary spent two full months with Jimmy. They went to Brookfield Zoo, the beach, and Shedd Aquarium. They took the world's fastest elevator to the top of Sears Tower. They had the time of their lives.

Alice saw her grandson, Tony, for a total of ten hours all year.

Why was the long-distance grandmother able to spend so much more time with her grandson? Because she has such a good relationship with her daughter. They enjoy being together. Her daughter feels that it's important for Jimmy to get to know his grandmother, so she readily grants Mary access to Jimmy.

Alice and her son, however, are still struggling with the pain he caused her during his teenage years. He abused alcohol and drugs. And even though he's been clean for seven years, Alice just cannot forgive him. Their troubled relationship is an enormous barrier to Alice's grandparenting. During the summer, Alice repeatedly invites little Tony to her house. But she makes it a point to invite only her grandson—not her son. Hurt, he angrily tells his mother that if he is not good enough for her, his son isn't either.

Let's face it. Our children control our access to our grandchildren. When we keep our relationship with our children healthy, working hard to clear up old issues and deal quickly and reasonably with current problems, our access to our beloved grandchildren will never be threatened or limited.

Attitudes. Our children also control attitudes. Their attitudes toward us, if expressed to their children, will exert a huge influence on how our grandchildren feel about us. If our children regard us with suspicion and mistrust, our grandchildren will almost certainly feel the same way toward us.

The power to determine attitudes may be even more important than access. As grandparents we can usually win the right to see the children, even if it means going to court. But we cannot dictate the attitudes our children have toward us. Nor can we control what our children say about us to our grandchildren. I have known parents who continually disparage their parents—more accurately, one set of parents—to the grandchildren. These impressionable young minds become filled with negative images of Grandma and Grandpa. Your children and their spouses have great power in directing your grandchildren's affections.

When we recognize the power our children have over our relationship to our grandchildren, we may respond in one of two unproductive ways. We may become angry and defensive, or we may become too eager to please our children. These behaviors will not help our cause as creative grandparents. One parent said to me, "The only reason my mother is nice to me is because she's afraid that if she treats me like she always has, I won't let her see the children. She was always sharp-tongued and critical. Now she's so icky sweet I can't stand it!"

Your children aren't stupid. They'll see right through your behavior to your motives. If your relationship with your son has been difficult in the past, and following the arrival of a new grandchild you suddenly try to dive into his life as if nothing has happened, he'll know what you're up to. He'll still have his anger and resentment from the past to deal with. We can't start the relationship with our children brand-new, forgetting all that has gone on before, just because we now have a grandchild.

The onset of grandparenting, however, does present a wonderful opportunity to improve our relationship with our adult children. This letter we received from a thirty-two-year-old man named Bill illustrates the point.

> Dad and I didn't get along very well while I was in high school and college. In fact, that's putting it mildly. I always felt like Dad expected too much of me. I had to be a great athlete. I had to get A's. I had to be a perfect Christian. I just couldn't do it.
>
> So I spent a lot of time rebelling against my Dad, and in a lot of ways I acted like a jerk to him. You know, just mean whenever I thought I could get away with it. Over the years our relationship has kind of steadied out, with him tolerating me and me not yelling at him. But we really have never come to terms with our past. I didn't think it was possible.
>
> Until my daughter was born. She is my parent's first grandchild. It was weird, but as I stood over Marissa's crib, I began to understand my father. I realized that the hopes and fears I have for my daughter are similar to those he had for me. And watching him with Marissa, I see a side of him, a gentleness, that I had never seen before. I went to my Dad the other day, and for the first time in years I asked him for advice. I thought he was going to fall over! But a smile came over his face and we talked, I mean really talked, for the first time in ten years.

Wise, creative grandparents do not see their children as obstacles to their happiness, but as people who need love, patient understanding, and support. Some grandparents love their grandchildren at the expense of their children. No good! It's an easy trap to fall into, especially if they have struggled with their feelings about their own adult children. They may see them as no longer needing their approval. Nothing could be further from the truth!

So far we have been assuming that the relationship between grandparents and parents is not particularly good. Now the other side. Grandparents who enjoy the love, trust, and respect of their children are much more likely to receive those same feelings from their grandchildren. My self-appointed role as "greatest grandfather in the world" comes not only from the time I spend with them, but also from what spin my children give to me and my actions as they discuss them with their children. I am grateful that my boys love and respect me. I have no doubt that the good relationship I have with my grandchildren started with my relationship with my sons.

Because we know how important our children are to our creative grandparenting opportunities, we must treat our children with love and respect—especially in front of our grandchildren. Sadly, that often does not happen. Frankly, I've often missed the boat on this point. Sometimes I think my wife, Judy, and I could have written a book titled, *How to Embarrass and Anger Your Children*. If you would like to really mess up your relationship with your children, poisoning their attitudes and forcing them to restrict the time you spend with your grandchildren, here are some suggestions.

1. Parent your grandchildren. Works every time. Nothing upsets your children more than when you step into their role. You're the grandparent. Become parent, and you've robbed your children of their job—and their right and responsibility before God. Make sure, for example, to interfere when they discipline. Tell your grandchild that you'd have never put them in "time out" for that. Hang over your children's shoulders when they parent. Sigh heavily whenever you disagree with their policies. Act as if the responsibility of raising the children were yours. I'm sure your children, like mine, will really appreciate becoming helpless bystanders in the lives of their own children!

2. Usurp your children's authority. Another way to say a quick good-bye to good feelings between you and your children is to violate their authority. If they tell you that their children are not allowed to have snack before dinner, ignore what they say and buy them an ice cream cone. The bigger the better. After all, you and I are the real grown-ups, right? We know better than our children. I know they are adults and all that, but without us they'd never let the grandchildren have any fun. Without us, they would fail miserably as parents. (It might be a good idea to let them know you feel this way.)

3. Criticize them publicly. If parenting your grandchildren isn't enough to really anger your children, then criticizing them in front of others is sure to do the trick. You don't have to be obnoxious about it. Just let it be known that you feel they have a lot to learn as parents. Give them the impression that you have all the answers. The key here is to do it in front of their friends or, even better, in front of the children. Do as much as you can to undermine their credibility with your grandchildren. "Grandpa really knows better than your dad, so listen to him."

For some mysterious reason, this produces violent mood swings in your son or daughter. "Now, Son, I can't believe you let the children go outside in weather like this without their hats. And look at their coats! How long since you've washed them? If you don't have enough money for winter coats, just let me know and I'll . . . ." A few sentences like that and we'll never have to worry about seeing our grandchildren again.

4. One-up your children in love. Another good way to antagonize your children is to help them see how much more you love their children than they do. Of course, it might be necessary to spend a little money to bribe your grandchildren with candy, clothes, and toys. Take a few months to prepare for the big moment. Finally it comes. You trot the grandchildren into the living room before a large family gathering and ask with a loud voice, "Now who do you children love best? Mom or Grandma?" Parents are always delighted when their recently bribed children point to Grandma.

5. Keep the past alive. Another way to alienate your children is to remind them about how bad they were to you when they were children. Constantly remind them about their past failures. Never let them forget the times they hurt you. Imply that you would have had a much easier life without them. Tell of the pain they brought into your life. If you do, I'll guarantee that grandparenting will never occupy much of your time. Your children, and by default your grandchildren, will avoid you like the plague. And they should!

Understanding your relationship with your children
Peter was sixteen the first time he really had it out with his parents. It seemed like a little thing to them, no big deal. Peter had come home from school filled with excitement about his grade in a creative writing class. Not only

had his teacher given him an A, she had told Peter quite enthusiastically that with his talent and imagination, he should consider becoming a writer.

Peter ran through the front door to tell his parents the good news. "Mom, Mrs. Burdick thinks I could be a writer. She really likes my story. I think that's what I'd like to major in at college—writing."

"Now calm down, Peter. What are you talking about? You know your father has his heart set on your becoming a mechanical engineer. We've discussed this before, and it's all decided. With your abilities in math and science, it would be foolish for you to try anything as uncertain as writing. You know most writers never earn very much money, and they have to work in restaurants as waiters and dishwashers. Look, here comes your father."

"Bill, talk to Peter. He's come home with some crazy idea that he wants to major in journalism and become a writer."

"A writer, Peter? What's gotten into that thick head of yours? You can't waste your life like that. You're going to be an engineer, and you're going to be a darn good one. If you think I'm going to pay for you to go to college to become a writer, you've got another think coming. The free ride lasts only as long as you listen to us."

Peter protested, but it was no use. It was clear that his parents had his future already planned for him. He became angry and said some things he didn't mean. They grounded Peter and took his car away from him for two months.

Peter did not become a writer. He is busy right now at the computer in his office as a mechanical engineer. It has been eleven years since he graduated from college, and his parents are extremely proud of him. But Peter is not happy as an engineer. He is still angry with his parents. He feels that it was not fair for them to use their financial support of his education to hold him hostage. He's afraid that it's too late for him to change now. He has a wife and two little girls, and they are purchasing a home. But late at night, while the family is asleep, Peter still thinks about writing. His anger and resentment are growing with his unfulfilled dreams.

Peter is dealing with two issues that will deeply color his relationship with his parents for the rest of his life: loyalty and justice. In his experience they are in conflict. You and I must face these same two issues if we are to understand our relationship with our children.

Peter feels indebted to his family for all they have done for him. They loved him, they encouraged him in school, and they paid for his college education. His father even helped him get his first engineering position. Peter's sense of *loyalty* to his parents, however, collides with his sense of *justice*. He feels that even though his parents did so much for him, ultimately they were not fair with him. Everything they did for him had strings attached. They used it to control him.

Loyalty and justice are difficult issues for Peter to work through. When he dwells on the injustice he feels from his past, his sense of loyalty is undermined and he feels guilty and angry. He cannot let himself admit that his parents were not being fair with him. His sense of loyalty gets in the way. How could he be disappointed and angry with parents who made such great sacrifices for him? The result is confusion in his attitudes toward his mom and dad. Even though he feels indebted to his parents, he feels there are some things they also owe him.

When we become grandparents, old conflicts between justice and loyalty often come to the forefront. Looking back, I can see where these issues were problems for me and my children. So can you, I'll wager. We may not have pushed our son into an engineering career, but we have done and said other things that affect their feelings of loyalty and justice.

Perhaps you can see how your relationship with your children has produced conflicting feelings of loyalty and justice. They saw you as cold and demanding, even though in your heart you didn't feel that way. Your daughter may feel that you favored a sibling over her. Or you were so busy "putting food on the table" that you didn't have time for your children, and they are still angry about that today. It's even possible that you physically or emotionally mistreated your child, creating an immense conflict in their minds between loyalty and justice.

Chances are that you and I did not realize what was happening in the minds of our children. We were all caught up in doing our best with all the facets of our lives, and we wanted the best for them. It does little good to look back with regret and wish we could do it all over again. The point here is to analyze where loyalty and justice may have come into conflict in our children and how it affects our relationship with them—and ultimately with our grandchildren. Make no mistake! It affects our grandparenting today, whether we admit it or not. Thus, we have some serious and important work to do.

One grandparent abused his children physically. He would get drunk and hit them. While they were in high school, he sought help for his alcoholism and eventually stopped drinking. When the drinking ended, the abuse ended. But his children remember. They are still angry with him. It wasn't fair that Dad hit them, especially when they sensed that it was to act out his own anger and not because of anything they did. Through it all, as children do, they still loved him. But now, when the family gets together, they shield the grandchildren from him. They remember all too clearly the drunken rages and violence of their childhood, and they unconsciously are protecting their children from him. He has six grandchildren he cannot know well because of the injustice and fear his children still feel.

Every relationship has a set of books, almost like a business account. This ledger has debits, credits, and a balance. Our children are constantly making entries into that set of books. Loyalty is on one side; justice is on the other. At some point, often when they become parents, our children bring the books forward for an audit. If justice and loyalty don't balance, it will have a profound effect on our grandparenting.

William is thirty-five. He has struggled all his life with the high expectations of his super-achiever parents. He was never as driven as they are. William manages a convenience store. He does not make a lot of money, but his marriage is solid and his life is relatively stress-free. Even so, his parents make no secret of their disappointment in him.

Then William's daughter was born. For the first time, he had done something that made his parents proud. He had never been able to meet their expectations—until now. He gave them their first granddaughter—the first girl born into the family for three generations—and they are proud of him. William had always felt that he owed his parents, that he had not done enough to justify their investment in him. With the birth of little Jennie, the ledger was finally balanced. As a matter of fact, as he watched his stern, driven father giggle with his granddaughter, William realized that the scales had tipped in his favor. Now they owed him, and it felt good.

William's parents are going to be involved grandparents. He is going to grant them easy access, and his attitude toward their involvement in his daughter's life is good. He feels better about himself when he sees how happy his parents are when they play with Jennie. Loyalty and justice have come together, although not perfectly, making creative grandparenting possible.

Sue is also thirty-five, but her story is different. Her world was rocked by the birth of her twins. They were her first children—her parents' first grandchildren. Sue carries a lot of anger around from her childhood. Her father is a workaholic who took time away from his children to make a lot of money. He loved her, sure, but he never showed her his love through words or physical touch. He seemed distant and uncaring to Sue.

But now Sue's dad is over all the time. This cold, unloving man is completely enthralled by his granddaughters. Yet as Sue watches him make such a fuss over them, she is angry. Why didn't he give her attention like that? Why didn't he ever show her the affection he so readily lavishes on her girls? And why does he still treat her as if she were invisible?

Sue finally couldn't take it any longer. She informed her father that he was no longer welcome in her home. She told him that he wasn't a very good influence on the girls. She chose to sabotage his relationship with his grandchildren without telling him the reason. He is angry with her for cheating him out of his grandchildren; she is furious with him for cheating her of his affection and himself while she was a child.

Now, Sue does not feel right about what she's doing. She does not enjoy using her girls as a pawn in her relationship with her father. She feels guilty about her strong negative feelings toward her dad, but that only makes her all the more angry. As a result, family visits are rare and tense. As Sue's children grow, they will feel the tension. They will be uncomfortable around their grandfather without knowing why.

We have discussed several relationships where reconciliation is essential. Will it happen? It seems impossible. But you *can* resolve old hurts. You can create a balance between justice and loyalty. The next section will show you how to get started.

The road to reconciliation

Peter and Sue's parents want to know what they can do to bring an end to the cycle of anger, bitterness, and guilt their children are experiencing. You and I want to bring healing to our own fragile relationships. We long to be free to grandparent creatively. Before we can do that, however, we have to reconcile with our children. But we don't know how.

The tendency is to blame our children for our feelings. After all, we did our best, we tried our hardest. We sincerely believe it isn't our fault that our children misread our intentions or were hurt by our expectations. They should have known how we really felt.

If we continue to point the finger of blame and responsibility at them, we will never achieve reconciliation. At best we can hope for an uneasy truce, forced on us by our impressionable grandchildren. But it does not have to be that way! The sooner we realize that we cannot control the actions of our children, and the sooner we accept responsibility for our part in the conflict and the healing, the sooner we'll be able to get on with the business of creative grandparenting.

As parents and grandparents intent on rebuilding our relationships with our children and forging strong relationships with our grandchildren, it's time to close out all outstanding accounts. It's time to balance the books and slam the covers of that dusty old ledger together with a resounding thump!

In the hit movie *Home Alone*, eight-year-old Kevin finds himself sitting in church beside his elderly neighbor, a bedraggled old man who is the subject of frightening rumors among the neighborhood children. The man is there during a Christmas choir rehearsal because he knows he wouldn't be welcome during the performance. Years before, he and his son had a longstanding grievance that had erupted into harsh words and flailing fists. The old man was not allowed to see his beautiful granddaughter, so he sneaked in when he wouldn't be noticed. Sensing his anguish and pain, Kevin asked him this simple question, "Why don't you just go to your son and tell him you're sorry?" The old man mumbled that it wasn't that simple and sidled away.

The first step on the road to reconciliation really *is* that simple. To begin the process of reconciliation, follow Kevin's sage advice and *go to your children*. This first step will probably be the most difficult. It takes humility and courage to lose face. The producers of *Home Alone* probably did not know it, but they were giving biblical advice. According to Matthew 18, the first step to reconciliation is to go to the person one-on-one. And Matthew 5:23 says that if you know someone has something against you, go to that person and reconcile it before you offer your gifts to the Lord.

The Scriptures are clear: Go to your children. Go, even if you feel they have done you wrong. Go, even if it means setting aside your pride. Go, even if you are certain they are more to blame than you are. Your relationship with them, and with your precious grandchildren, is far more important than a stubborn question of who did what to whom. Take the first step toward reconciliation. Go to your children.

When you go, take the next step and *acknowledge past mistakes*. Now is the time to say, "I was wrong. I realize it now. I am sorry." Now is the time to admit that you failed at times. Now is the time to agree that you sometimes did the wrong thing. Remind them that parenting is hard. They should begin to understand, because now they are parents too.

When we have come this far, we might expect our children to make a big move toward us. Don't! After all, it may have taken you ten years to figure out where you went wrong. It may take them another ten to see where they were wrong. Don't be hurt if, when you acknowledge your mistakes, they don't rush to you with open arms and tearful celebration. Deep hurts take a long time to heal. By taking these two steps to begin the healing process, you are doing the right thing.

Let your children know that in admitting your failures, you are not expecting anything in return. If you get it, wonderful! But this is not a game of *quid pro quo*. Your painful disclosure and apology may be met with suspicion or indifference. That's okay. You have done your part. "He who conceals his sins does not prosper, but whoever confesses and renounces them finds mercy" (Prov. 28:13). This principle applies to us as parents. We may not feel we have sinned, but we know that we have failed. Admit it, and ask for mercy. Forget about justice. God will take care of that. Go to your children with a gentle spirit and acknowledge your past mistakes.

The third step to reconciliation is to *accept God's forgiveness.* We must not beat ourselves up for past mistakes. The past is gone. Some things simply cannot be undone. We can't dive back twenty years and spend more time with our children. We can't take back angry words spoken long ago. We can't call back a hand loosed in anger. It's even too late for deep regrets. Know that God has forgiven all your failings, all your mistakes, all your sins. Because you have acknowledged your sins and failures and repented, God has reached down and touched you with His loving, forgiving hand. In Jesus Christ you have been forgiven.

Mary is gloomy all the time. She looks back on her fifty-nine years with regret and longing. She was not a very good parent. She was impatient, demanding, and quick to become angry. She screamed terrible words at her children. As a result, her relationships with her grown children are very poor. Mary has tried to forget the past, but it won't go away. She knows she was not a very good mom, yet she wants a chance to be a good grandparent. Her children are learning to forgive her, and they are rediscovering one another. But Mary is not fun to be around because she will not forgive herself. She dwells on her past failings constantly. It seems to be all she thinks about. She longs to reclaim the lost years, but she can't go back. And she is missing her grandchildren's wonder years because she will not let herself accept the loving forgiveness of God.

In her book *Traits of a Healthy Family*, Delores Curran points out that healthy families are not afraid to ask for help. If the problems between you and your children are so deep, and the misunderstandings so pronounced that you no longer feel capable of resolving the conflict alone, don't give up. Ask for help. When we are confronted by obstacles that seem insurmountable, the answer is to look outside ourselves for assistance.

The first place we should turn is often our last resort. Don't wait until it's too late to ask God to intervene in your relations with your children. He is our best resource! The Bible speaks repeatedly of the power of prayer. As you seek reconciliation by going to your children, acknowledging past mistakes, and accepting God's forgiveness, make prayer an important part of the process. Ask God for help.

Ask other family members for help. Don't let them gang up on your son or daughter, but consider using them as an intermediary. If every discussion between you and your daughter turns ugly, perhaps your son can be a calming influence. Family members can be valuable resources in bringing reconciliation to the family.

You might also want to consider your pastor or church as a source of help. Churches should be a first-line source of support and safety during the stress and uncertainty of reconciliation. Pastors and church friends can be a source of tremendous encouragement to you. They will pat you on the back for going down the difficult path of reconciliation, hugging you when things don't go well and rejoicing with you when the relationship is restored. The key is to let someone know what is going on. Be wise, of course, and discreet. Tell that trusted church person the truth and let them know you need their support and prayers. You cannot do it alone, and you don't have to. Don't let shame or embarrassment rob you of the loving, confidential support of your pastor and friends.

Finally, if you cannot find reconciliation any other way, look to a trained family counselor for help. He or she can help you understand your past and how it affected your parenting. He can put your present relationships in perspective. A good counselor can give you wise insight and help you form a plan for working through the hurts and pain of the past.

Rethinking the process

You and your sons and your daughters: The single biggest factor in your grandparenting career is your relationship with them. Don't minimize its importance. Take the lead. Be proactive. Look for ways to improve your children's attitudes toward you. Look for opportunities to build up and bless your children. Remember, a parent's relationship with his or her adult children does not take care of itself. Tend that relationship, not only because you should and want to, but knowing that your grandparenting depends on it. Take the risks involved to reconcile with your children. Don't despair of ever becoming a creative, involved grandparent. Do the right thing; seek reconciliation. Don't let pride stand in your way. Your grandchildren need you. Do it for them, for yourself, and for the Lord.

The path to creative grandparenting goes through your children. They are the means of access, and their attitudes are vitally important. Are you making some mistakes in your grandparenting? Running through some stop signs? Assuming too much authority and taking too much control out of your children's hands? Step back.

Relax. Talk openly with your children about what you may be doing wrong and what they expect. Communicate openly, honestly, painfully, lovingly.

And if you can grandparent only a little, or if access is denied because of strained or broken relationships with your children, get to work on it. Take the enormous risks involved in moving toward reconciliation. Do your part. God will do His; He always does. Then be patient as the door of access to those precious grandchildren who need you so very much is gradually opened.

Quiz for creative grandparents

Yes/No   I respect my children for their parenting efforts.

Yes/No   If my grandchildren lived with me they'd be better off.

Yes/No   I recognize that my evaluation of their parenting might be unrealistic.

Yes/No   When a parent and child are in conflict, the child is always responsible to make the first move toward reconciliation.

Yes/No   The kind of parenting I did will not affect my children's parenting.

Yes/No   I honestly feel that I love my grandchildren more than their parents do.

Yes/No   I can see how my parenting sometimes produced a conflict between loyalty and justice in my children

Yes/No   I recognize that reconciliation is a process, not a one-time deal.

Yes/No   I am willing to take a reality check of my grandparenting by asking my children to tell me honestly how I am doing.

Chapter Seven

Involvement Versus Interference

Zelda is feeling pretty good about herself. On her own initiative she went to the local cycle shop and picked out a beautiful pink bicycle for her five-year-old granddaughter, Beka. It wasn't easy deciding which bike to purchase. Zelda had looked long and hard. Not just any bicycle would do. Beka was special, vivacious, full of love and kinetic energy. Searching for a bike that matched Beka's personality was a long and exhaustive task. At last Zelda found it, complete with streamers and a picture of a golden-haired girl on the bar. Zelda didn't hesitate. She pulled out her credit card and took the bike home that day.

True, Beka already had a bike, but to Zelda it wasn't good enough. The old bike had a low tire, torn seat, and rusty handlebars—a dilapidated hand-me-down. Beka has been asking her mom for a new bike, but she's been told there just isn't any money. Zelda knew that she would be Beka's hero for buying the bike. So, on a bright Saturday in May, Grandma Zelda presented her surprised and thrilled granddaughter with her new bicycle. The huge smile and big bear hug were well worth the time, energy, and $125 she had invested. Grandma returned home glowing, a hero to her granddaughter.

Donna, Zelda's daughter, is not thrilled. Being a single mom is tough. Money has been tight since the divorce. Her job barely provides food, clothes, and a roof over her and her two daughters' heads. Extras like a new bike just aren't possible. Beka has been asking for a bike all spring. Donna really wishes that she could afford it, but the money just isn't there. Trying to explain that to Beka wasn't easy. In the end Beka had run off to her room crying, "You don't love me! You're a mean mom."

Then Grandma came riding to the rescue, like the cavalry in a John Wayne movie. Just as Beka was beginning to understand that her bike could be fixed for a few dollars, that she didn't need all kinds of new things, that earning money for food and paying the bills were part of real life, in came Grandma. Donna was angry just thinking about it. How could her mother have spent $125 for a new bike that Beka really didn't need, when Donna was worried about paying the electric bill? Why didn't she ask first? Donna would have told her that she was trying to help Beka learn the value of money. It was important for her to understand that $125 is a lot of money; money that must be earned, and that could be spent on more important things.

To Donna, this was just one more example of her mother's interference. Ever since the divorce, under the guise of helping the family, her mom had been trying to parent her children. She bought them presents all the time, promised them a trip to Disneyland that Donna could never afford, and took them frequently for ice cream—all without asking her. Donna was frustrated and hurt. These were her girls, and she was losing them to her own mother. Whenever Mom had to say no, Grandma said yes. Now Beka and Lisa didn't even bother asking

Mom. They bypassed her and went right to the source of the bounty, Grandma. And Grandma Zelda rarely said no.

The line between being an involved, creative grand-parent and interfering with the parenting of your grand-children is easily crossed. As with Zelda and Donna, the perceptions of grandparents and parents often differ. Grandma thought she was helping out, being a good grandparent. Mom saw it as an intrusion into her territory as a parent. She felt threatened and angry.

In this chapter we will examine the issue of involve-ment versus interference. How can grandparents be cre-atively involved in the lives of their grandchildren without interfering with their parenting? To answer this question, we will look at the issues of discipline, lifestyle, expectations, and spoiling as they relate to interference and involvement. We will also suggest clear guidelines for grandparents who are eager to know where the invisible line between involvement and interference lies.

Discipline: not your problem!

Questions about disciplining children can provoke deep differences of opinion between parents and grandpar-ents. This issue presents a strong temptation for grand-parents to move beyond involvement to interference. It can be extremely painful for us to watch our children dis-cipline our grandchildren. They have different rules to govern their discipline than we did. When we raised chil-dren, spanking was commonplace. The maxim was: "Spare the rod, spoil the child." Today physical punish-ment has fallen into disrepute among child development experts. Our children, raised under corporal punishment, find themselves in the middle. On the one side are their parents, making dire predictions about alcohol and drug

abuse in children who grow up without "proper guidance." By "proper guidance," of course, grandparents usually mean spanking. On the other side of the issue are the
parenting professionals, who predict equally horrible
consequences for children who are spanked regularly.

As grandparents we say things like, "If you ever
talked like that to me when you were a child, I would
have taught you a thing or two." "Remember what I always told you, Son, 'I brought you into this world and I
can take you out.'" "I tell you what—you had respect for
me, not like that disrespectful teenager of yours." If we
feel that our children are too permissive in their parenting style, we may not be shy about letting them know it.
Our motives are pure. We want our grandchildren to
grow up to be terrific human beings. But we think our
way is the only way to achieve that.

But the issue could also be deeper and more malig-
nant. We may be trying to control our grown children.
We may be much more interested in getting them to do
our thing than the right thing. It feels like a slap in the
face, like a renouncing of our methods, when our child's
parenting style differs from ours. This is especially true if
they appear to be successful. We are hurt and a little angry; they feel rejected and unappreciated.

One sad grandparent expressed his feelings this way;
"Was I such a horrible parent, spanking my children?
They turned out all right. But now, he acts as if his children are too precious to spank. I bet my son thinks I was
too hard on him. But I did my best. Why can't he do it the
way he was brought up?" This grandparent is afraid that
his children resent their childhood. This makes him question his parenting. In his insecurity he may become even
more determined to prove that his way is the right way.

Sometimes we make our disapproval known in no uncertain terms to our grandchildren. Huge mistake! "Johnny, your mom and dad sure let you get away with a lot more than I ever would. Why, if you were my son, I'd let you know who was boss. I'm not your dad, and you can't get away with that stuff with me."

If we feel that our children should have been tougher, we heave a big sigh and mutter under our breath, just loud enough for everyone to hear, "I guess the times have changed, but I wonder . . . ."

But there's another side to the issue of discipline. Sometimes we feel that our child is being too tough on our grandchildren. The urge is to jump into the middle of the fray and act as the family referee. This vote of no confidence is a sure way to enrage your children and confuse your grandchildren.

On occasion it may be proper and even necessary to intervene on your grandchild's behalf. In instances of physical or sexual abuse, for example, grandparents not only have a right but also a responsibility to act in the best interests of the children and remove them from danger. They may even have to go to the extreme of reporting their own children to the proper authorities. For most grandparents, however, the issue is not abuse. Instead, it is a parent raising her voice, losing her temper, punishing rather than disciplining. As grandparents, we need to remember that we are not full-time members of the household. We haven't seen what has gone before. If Jill has missed her curfew six straight weekends in a row and we only catch Mom losing it on the sixth weekend, we are not seeing the whole picture.

Remember, grandparents are a step removed from the parenting process. Parents are responsible to look at their long-term goals for their children. They want them to become functioning, valuable members of society. Grandparents goals, however, can be more selfish and more quickly obtained. We are looking for the quick hug and bright smile. But the look of love for Grandma or the smile for Grandpa does not come through discipline. The short-term pain brought into our grandchildren's lives by their parent's discipline hurts us too. Even though we know in our heads that in the long term it is beneficial, our hearts betray us and we move in to interfere and prevent the short term pain. This is understandable. But it's also understandable that our children are not going to serenely let us interfere with their parenting.

So our children find themselves between the proverbial immovable object (us) and the irresistible force (their parental responsibility). They become confused and afraid. Interfering with the parenting of our grandchildren may make us feel more in control or more important, but it only damages our fragile relations with our children and makes their job more difficult. When we step in, we are sending a loud message that our child is not capable of parenting on his own. And the parents are not the only ones who receive this message. Our grandchildren soon observe the contempt we show toward their parents. This makes discipline all the more difficult. Usually our stated goal is to help our children parent better. Ironically, our interference actually sabotages our children's effectiveness.

Angie is sixteen. By most standards, she is a good kid. She does well in school, she doesn't do drugs, she doesn't drink. Angie does have a long-term relationship with her boyfriend. It irritates her parents that she would rather be with him than with them. Angie is allowed to see her boyfriend on weekends and one night a week. Her parents, Valerie and Doug, have just found out that she has been sneaking out to see him after they go to bed on weeknights. They are angry and afraid. Angry that she has lied to them and deceived them; afraid that she is sexually involved with her boyfriend. The whole situation came to a head when Grandpa and Grandma were in town, visiting for the week. Mom and Dad caught Angie crawling back into her window, and the ensuing scene woke Grandma. She put on her old housecoat and went to investigate the cause of the midnight ruckus. When Grandma heard the story, she laughed out loud and said to Valerie, "Remember when you used to sneak out of the house to be with Tommy Herman? I knew the whole time what you were doing, but I never said a word. Now, why don't you just let Angie get to sleep and leave her alone?" Valerie was furious. She felt it right to ground Angie for a month, and now Angie was laughing at her with Grandma. Valerie had lost control of the situation. Her mother had ruined her credibility with Angie, not by disclosing her youthful foibles, but by treating Valerie's indignation and anger as unimportant. Valerie knew that Grandma's reaction would be used as ammunition in their next battle over boyfriends.

Angie's grandmother had stepped beyond involvement to interference. Yet to this day she tells that story with pride. She really thinks the embarrassed look that came over her daughter's face was funny, and she is convinced that she saved Angie from a grave injustice. Last Christmas, Grandma told the story to the entire family, much to the delight of almost everyone present. She thought Valerie was being a little too dramatic when she stomped from the room, followed by the laughter of the family. This grandmother had not learned how to keep from interfering with discipline.

The rule is simple: Discipline is not our problem. Whenever we offer unsolicited advice on our children's disciplinary actions, we have overstepped our bounds. Bite your tongue. Your children are going to make mistakes. Ours do too (at least by my preachy standards). They need to learn on their own, just as we did. If you give your children the freedom to discipline as they see fit without hounding them into doing it your way, they may even come to you for the very advice that you want so dearly to give them. If you force your advice and wisdom on them, they will resent it, and you.

Not very long ago, my son asked me this question; "Dad, do you think I'm too hard on my children?" Jack was concerned that his discipline, although very rarely corporal, was too harsh. He wondered if he was expecting too much. It was reassuring and affirming for him when I was able to say, "No, Jack. You're doing a great job, I think you're a terrific dad." If Judy and I had forced him to follow our thinking on discipline, or made him look foolish in front of his children, he may never have given us the opportunity to comment on his parenting.

Don't push your children away. Discipline is not your problem. Any attempt to make it your responsibility without being asked will produce pain and hard feelings.

Expectations: too high or too low?

Bill did not finish high school. Although he is now retired at sixty-five, he used to work ten- to twelve-hour days to scratch out a living for his wife and two sons. Bill wanted something better than the steel mills for his boys, so he was tough on them, especially when it came to school work. They were expected to do well in school, because Bill wanted his sons to go to college. His lifelong dream was that they would have a better life than him. They were bright boys, and they loved their father. They did what they were told. Both of Bill's sons went on to medical school. One became a surgeon, the other an anesthesiologist. Both of Bill's boys had sons of their own, and he loves his grandsons.

But now Bill is angry. Joe, his oldest grandson has just reluctantly shown Grandpa his report card. He had earned two B's, three C's and a D. Grandpa was furious. He walked over to his son and asked, "Did you see that boy's horrible report card? He should be grounded. Did you tell him he has to do better next time?"

"Dad, I talked to Joe, and he really tried his best. He is not a student, and he probably never will be. I don't really care what grades he gets as long as he does his best."

"Does his best?" Grandpa thundered. "It is obvious to me that the boy is just lazy. He's fifteen and you treat him like he's still a baby. I'm telling you, he isn't going to amount to anything."

Bill angered his son and his daughter-in-law by interfering with their parenting. But that's not all. He nearly broke his grandson's heart, because Joe had overheard most of Grandpa's tirade. Bill insists that he didn't step over the line. He blames his son for not expecting enough from Joe.

Our ideals as grandparents can cause us to interfere in the parenting of our grandchildren. We look for them to complete developmental tasks, such as walking and talking, early. We have high standards for their behavior, both public and private. We have special dreams for their future. We know what kind of people we want them to grow up to be, and what we think they should do with their lives.

These expectations are often our little secret. We don't let anyone in on them. They are hidden from view, they crystallize slowly, and they appear without our making a conscious effort to form them. Once in place, however, they are a powerful force in our grandparenting.

Nothing is wrong with having ideals for your grandchildren. That's natural. The problems occur when our hopes become unreasonable and rigid expectations.

We have two grandchildren who were verbal very early, and two who did not talk clearly until later. By coincidence, it was the first grandchild who spoke early and clearly. We were delighted to listen to her jabber around the house. At two years of age, Lauren recited all of *The Night Before Christmas*. We couldn't believe it! We were convinced that she was the smartest little girl in the world. Then Erin came along, and at three she was talking like a teenager. We decided that we had the two smartest grandchildren in the world. Their verbal skills created within us the expectation that all of our grandchildren would develop early. We were wrong. As toddlers, Jonathon and Elena were not nearly as verbal as Lauren and Erin. Our expectations were out of line with reality. Some children simply talk earlier than others, and it has little to do with intelligence.

Many grandparents spend a lot of time bragging about their grandchildren. It's their favorite pastime. Sometimes these sessions become competitive.

"My grandson walked at eleven months. I heard that your grandson didn't walk until he was thirteen months old. What was wrong with him?"

"Well, he didn't walk until thirteen months but he knew *Hamlet* by heart when he was three."

"My granddaughter walked out of the womb quoting the Bible. . . ."

You get the idea. These exchanges between grandparents and friends create developmental expectations that no child could live up to. So we respond by pushing the parents. We ask our children if they have considered a speech therapist because in our minds, two-year-olds who don't talk well are already behind. We try to get the children to walk to us at six months of age. We nag our child about any marginal lack of development. We worry about whether our grandchildren are being potty-trained soon enough, and if they wet the bed we worry that they will do so forever. We're concerned that our daughters and daughters-in-law are nursing their babies too long. If the child isn't on a schedule, we worry about that too.

If we kept our expectations to ourselves, we would probably be okay. But most of us feel the need to share our concerns with our children, and somehow we share them repeatedly and often. In the process we create frustration and anger. We shame our children, and we make them embarrassed for their children. What is even worse, we are putting enormous weight on tiny shoulders.

Being toilet-trained at twelve, eighteen, or twenty-four months does not determine whether our grandchildren are going to be successful in life. I'm sure there are corporate executives who didn't know The Night Before Christmas at two years of age. Don't rush your grandchildren. They will grow up soon enough.

Grandparents also have high expectations for behavior. One grandfather refused to take his children out to dinner because they were very young, wiggly, and loud.

He was embarrassed by toddlers who did not live up to his lofty expectations. Little children cannot sit quietly for very long, and their parents are not neglecting their duty. You can't punish toddlers for acting like toddlers. Yet we often hear grandparents in restaurants complaining to their children because their young grandchildren are not living up to their expectations. "Debbie, can't you keep your kids quiet? For crying out loud, everyone in the restaurant is looking at us. Now be quiet, Jason. Please be quiet . . . ." Of course, it is at that point that Jason slides out of his high chair and takes off at full speed. Instead of spending your time being embarrassed and angry, do what you can to entertain them or choose a family restaurant next time. That's the creative, involved way to grandparent.

We want our teenage grandchildren to conform to adult standards of behavior. We expect them to act like "young gentlemen and ladies." This is not unreasonable, except that what we usually mean is, "Don't act like an American teenager." We're shocked when they slouch past us in torn jeans and a rock music T-shirt. "Jill, did you see what Bobby is wearing? I can't believe you let him wear that shirt. I would never have let you out of the house looking like that."

My wife's mother used to wonder if Jack respected Judy and me because of the way he spoke to us. When Jack was about thirteen he called me Pops. Once, in his grandmother's presence, he made fun of my receding hairline by calling me Baldy. His grandma was aghast that we would let our children speak to us that way. "Judy, don't you think that's a funny way for him to talk to Jerry?" My wife, who knew the deep bond that Jack and I share, said no. She thought it was a sign of a good relationship that Jack would kid me like that. Still Grandma persisted. "But if anyone heard him talk to Jerry like that, what would they think?" Grandma was missing the point. She was interfering in our parenting. What she was really saying was, "You are not doing a good enough job raising your son. You are not teaching him to respect you. His behavior does not live up to my expectations."

Perhaps we are most concerned about the future of our grandchildren. Because we want the best for them (and us), we develop expectations that suffocate our children and our grandchildren. You met Bill a few pages back. Bill is not a lousy grandfather. As a matter of fact, Bill is a creative, involved grandfather. But his expectations for his grandchildren are causing him to interfere loudly and obnoxiously. Is Bill wrong to want the best for his grandchildren? Of course not. But Bill steps over the line in the way he communicates his ideals. He has developed rigid and unrealistic expectations. His grandchildren will never be able to measure up to them. What is Bill going to do if his oldest grandson decides he wants to pick raspberries for a living? Is he going to disown him? Will he stay angry at the parents indefinitely? Bill's expectations and his interference will inevitably limit his grandparenting opportunities. That would be the real tragedy, not a grandson who picks raspberries.

Our children will resent our intrusion if we force our expectations onto their parenting. It drives a wedge into our relationship with our children. The guideline for dealing with your ideals is this: *Don't lock your children and grandchildren into your expectations.* Let them grow and develop into the human beings God wants them to be, with their own unique gifts, skills, and personalities combining to make a wonderful creation.

Lifestyles: different isn't wrong.

Janey walks past Grandma Rose with her head bouncing and her body swaying. Grandma cannot ignore the music coming from Janey's portable CD player. The lyrics sound trashy to Grandma. Janey is wearing tight shorts and a sheer blouse. "Janey, Janey, JANEY!"

"Yes, grandmother¿"

"You're not going out on your date like that are you¿"

Janey laughs. She loves grandma and treasures spending time with her, but her grandmother is just so, well . . . old. "Sure, Grandma. It's not like I'm naked or anything. See ya later."

Rose shook her head. She wondered if she should bring it up to her children.

Janey seems so unsupervised. Her parents are too relaxed about her lifestyle. Grandma Rose had a horrible feeling that Janey and her boyfriend were . . . . well, you know, "doing it." She decided that the issue was too important to ignore, so she marched into her daughter's bedroom. "Barbara, did you see what Janey had on tonight¿ I'm sorry, but she looks like a, a . . . , well I can't even say it, but you know what I mean. And the music she listens to day and night is just plain immoral. Did I bring you up so bad that you ignore what your children are doing¿"

Lifestyle differences can be sources of deep irritation between parents and grandparents. Both are afraid the child is going off the deep end. The parent doesn't really want to be reminded of this fear. The grandparent may feel that the parent has somehow overlooked the blue mohawk haircut her teenage daughter is currently sporting. She feels the need to point it out, just in case. The result of this kind of interference is friction and guilt. The parents may not be happy about the lifestyles of their children, but they have already decided it's best not to try to change it. By harping on it, grandparents escape feeling guilty for not taking some kind of action.

Once again, this can be devastating. Angry parents can reduce our access to those grandchildren we love dearly and want to see, even if they do have blue hair.

An even more difficult situation arises when grandparents take issue with the lifestyle of the parent. One grandmother is exceedingly tidy. Well, tidy might be understating the case. The woman is positively eccentric about cleanliness. Her children, probably out of reaction to growing up in a surgically sterile environment, are not as clean. One of them is positively untidy. No, let's tell the truth. This guy is sloppy. And his wife accentuates, rather than alleviates, that quality in him.

Following the birth of their first child, Grandma came to help take care of the baby. Her son and his wife were apprehensive. They felt Grandma might have a few negative things to say about their laid-back way of life. They were wrong. She had *many* negative things to say about their lifestyle. "I can't believe you are going to bring a baby up in a place like this. You haven't scrubbed the floor in months, and your refrigerator is growing things. The baby. He'll probably get every disease known to mankind from the germs on your floor . . . ." Well, son and daughter-in-law could take only so much. So, on the fourth day of what was to have been a two-week visit, they ushered Grandma out the door and to the airport.

They purchased a first-class seat for her and gratefully watched her fly off.

Was Grandma right? Did her son need to be cleaner? I'm sure. Was she wrong in the way she handled it? You bet. And today, four years later, they are still angry with one another. The key phrase we must keep in mind when tempted to interfere with lifestyle is this: *It's their life, let them live it.* We want the best for our children and grandchildren, and we are convinced that we know exactly what is the best for them. Chances are that we've got it figured out a lot more completely than they do. But they are human beings, and ultimately they are responsible for making their own way in the world. They are free to decide what kind of people they want to be.

Let me illustrate. Jack was always more than a little willing to challenge the powers that be. He worried us. And the lifestyle decisions he made early in his adult life bothered us. Now, years later, his lifestyle has become very similar to ours. We are in ministry and writing this book together.

Our son Jon was the opposite. We knew he would be all right because he was very successful in high school and college. Jon was most like us in lifestyle during high school. Now an aeronautical engineer, Jon is an iconoclastic person. He has chosen a way of life quite different from Jack and me. Judy and I have learned (the hard way) to appreciate both sons and their differences from us. It's their life, let them live it. As much as we would like to, we cannot make lifestyle decisions for them. I know all about the urge to interfere. I feel it, and I have to fight it myself. But the rule is a good one. If we spend our time harping on nonessential things like hair and clothing, our children and grandchildren will be deaf to us when we need to speak to them about matters of true importance.

Spoiling: When is enough, enough?

The most frequent complaint about grandparents is that they spoil their grandchildren. Many grandparents tend to laugh it off. They feel or say aloud that a grandparent's job is to spoil her grandchildren. Often, we mean that we want to be free to give our grandchildren things we didn't give our children. But our son or daughter does not see it in such a favorable light. They see us as spoiling their children by giving them too much or giving them gifts that are too expensive.

The issue isn't really between you and your children. The real issue, although obscured by bickering and hurt feelings, is delayed gratification. Social scientists and child psychologists are pointing toward a new and disturbing trend in the personalities of today's young people. Children seem incapable of waiting for things. They want it all, they want it now, and they want it without sacrifice. M. Scott Peck, in *The Road Less Traveled*, pointed to this phenomenon as one of the roots of the selfishness and unhappiness of Americans.

Our grandchildren are being brought up in a world where sensuality is prominent and pleasure is the reigning pursuit. By *sensuality* I'm not speaking of sexuality, although sexuality is part of it. I'm speaking of indulging our senses, living at the mercy of the whims of our sensory feelings and emotions. That is the way of life for many of our grandchildren.

My granddaughter Lauren looks around the neighborhood and sees what is going on. More, she looks around and her seven-year-old eyes see what her friends are buying, wearing, and owning. And she wants it. This year, the grade-school rage was roller-blades. You've probably seen them. They look like roller skates, but the wheels are in line. They are very fast, very fun, very popular, and very expensive. So Lauren begged her father for roller blades.

"Dad, please. Dad, I can't go outside if I don't have roller blades. Please. . . ." Seven-year-olds have a way of putting on incredible pressure when they want something and feel they are being denied unfairly.

Her father was adamant. "Lauren, last year you had to have roller skates. This winter it was ice skates. I bought both of them for you. If you want roller blades, you will have to save your allowance and buy them with your own money,"

"But Dad, I need them now! Can't you just charge them? I'll pay you back later. I promise I'll never ask for anything again."

I spent some time with Lauren during her quest for roller blades. We hadn't been together three minutes when she asked me if we could go to the store and get roller blades. Judy and I love to buy things for our grandchildren. We love the look in their eyes when we bring a new gift to them and they just explode with joy. But this time I said no to Lauren. I knew it wasn't right without talking first to Jon and Lynn. Good thing I resisted Lauren's appeal! When I conferred with Jon he told me the story.

"Dad, Lauren was crying and throwing a fit because I wouldn't buy her roller blades. I told her she had to save up her own money and pay for them herself. She was almost out of control when I asked her to look at my shoes. I said, 'Lauren, how do my shoes look to you?' She said they looked terrible. I asked if she thought I should get new ones. She thought that, yeah, the time had definitely come for new shoes. These looked awful. Dad, then I looked in her eyes and asked how much new shoes would cost. She thought that I could probably buy them for about forty-five dollars. I asked her how much roller blades were. She replied, 'forty-five dollars.' Then I asked, 'Lauren, why haven't I bought new shoes?' She haltingly answered. 'Because you don't have the money.' I smiled and nodded my head and asked her why I wasn't buying roller blades. 'Because you don't have the money,' was the slow response.

"Dad, if you had bought her those roller blades, it would have messed up what I'm trying to do with Lauren. She thinks everything is hers for the taking—right now. And I'm trying to teach her that getting things comes through hard work, through doing what you don't want to do. Thank you for not interfering."

I learned a lot as I listened to that story. I realized, probably for the first time, that the key issue isn't spoiling. It is helping our children teach their children to become responsible adults. Responsible adults know how to delay gratification. You see, parents establish long-term goals for their children. You and I are usually thinking short-termed when we seek love and hugs from our grandchildren. We don't have to be as tough. And that's all right, as long as we don't compromise what our children are trying to accomplish.

Everything is permissible—but not everything is beneficial. Everything is permissible—but not everything is constructive. Nobody should seek his own good, but the good of others (1 Cor. 10:23-24).

Paul's point is well taken by creative grandparents. Spoiling is not constructive, it is not beneficial, and ultimately it is not for the good of others. Loving our grandchildren means that somehow we forego the fleeting pleasure of seeing them light up when we bring them a new treasure. We are willing to help build their character. They already have more than they will ever use. What children, youth, and young adults need is character, and careful, creative grandparents can help them along that path by refusing to interfere in matters of discipline, expectations, and lifestyle.

Checklist: involvement vs. interference

❑ It's important to me to please my grandchildren once in a while.

❑ A grandmother has a right to buy things for her grandchildren when they need them.

❑ My children are far too lenient with my grandchildren.

❑ If I didn't step in, they'd end up in jail.

❑ My grandchildren have a right to know when their parents are making a bad parenting mistake.

❑ When I override my children, it clarifies things for my grandchildren.

❑ My grandson is going to know how to ride a two-wheeler before he's three!

❑ I have an obligation to compare my expectations for my grandchildren with those of their parents.

❑ It's only right that my children establish the same house rules I had.

❑ If my children can't afford it and I can, I have every right to purchase it for my grandchildren.

❑ My grandchildren shouldn't have to wait for what they want, as long as I can get it for them.

Chapter Eight

Grandparenting With a Difference

"But you don't understand. My situation is different. We're not your typical mom, dad, and 2.5 children suburban family. I grew up in a small town Baptist church and married a local boy. But my twice-divorced son just married a Jewish girl from the Bronx, and she has two children from a previous marriage. How is an Indiana farm woman going to grandparent them? And now my son and his new wife are going to have a baby of their own."

The concerned grandmother went on. "Grandparenting for me is not like it was for my mother and grandmother. I can't assume, as they did, that my grandchildren are growing up with my values. Nor can I assume that I will be able to spend a lot of time with them. As a matter of fact, I don't have the slightest clue about how to relate to my new daughter-in-law. My instant grandchildren are six and ten, and they have grown up in New York City. When they came to visit last week, it was the first time in their lives that either of them had seen a real live cow or been to Sunday school. I'm not kidding when I say that I'm grandparenting with a difference!"

This grandmother has to face issues her grandparents would never have dreamed possible. Grandparents today must be ready to deal creatively with diverse reli-

gious backgrounds, ethnic dissimilarities, and a plethora
of family differences. Most of us prepare for grandparenting with the assumption that our children will grow up,
get married, have children, and live happily after. The reality for many families is that "happily ever after" never
happens.

In this chapter we will explain how to be creatively
involved in your grandchildren's lives when families are
different, when values are different, and when children
are different. Here are some examples.

• Jo is a fifty-eight-year-old African-American
grandmother whose pregnant daughter has just married a
white man. Jo wonders if her daughter is prepared to handle the ethnic and cultural differences in this marriage.

• Bill's daughter has been married three times. She
has four children by those marriages. She has just announced that she is moving in with her new boyfriend.
Bill is worried about his grandchildren's values, and he
wonders if his daughter understands the potential dam-
age she is doing.

• Ken, a grandfather of four, has just announced to
his children that he is divorcing their mother. He wonders how this will affect his relationship with his grandchildren.

• Sophia is a grandmother of six. She was the first
woman in her family to become a medical doctor. Most
of her goals for her children, and now her grandchildren,
center around their education. Sophia's daughter, who
has an MBA, recently married a man without a high
school diploma. This is a second marriage for both of
them. Sophia is afraid that his lack of education will have
a negative influence on her educational goals for her
grandchildren.

• Five years ago, Jim's son married a lovely girl who was not a Christian. Last week they brought Jim's first grandchild home from the hospital. Jim is worried that his son and daughter-in-law will not bring his grandson up to love Jesus.

• Reggie is five now, but you wouldn't be able to tell that by talking to him. Reggie is a special-needs child, developmentally disabled. Reggie's grandparents worry about how they will relate to a grandchild with whom they cannot communicate.

• Roger's grandson needs speech therapy. Mark, who is four years old, speaks only a few unclear words. The experts say that his frequent ear infections have resulted in slow speech development. Roger is concerned that his grandson isn't very smart. He's uncomfortable taking Mark out with him because he often has trouble knowing what Mark wants and what he is saying.

Each of the above situations calls for grandparenting with a difference. Ethnic and religious differences, blended families, and special-needs grandchildren present unique problems to involved, creative grandparents. Many men and women have met those special kinds of challenges without fear. As a result, they have had confident, joyful, and rewarding grandparenting experiences.

Here are six principles that will enable you to enjoy grandparenting with a difference.

1. Learn to live with your children's choices. Jo, our first grandmother, carries a great deal of anger toward her daughter. Although she prides herself on her lack of prejudice, she resents the fact that her daughter has put her in an awkward position. She hadn't expected to become a grandmother, and she hadn't thought about grandparenting a racially-mixed child. She is angry at her daughter and new son-in-law, and she is angry at herself for being upset with them. Jo has to learn the first principle of grandparenting with a difference. *She needs to learn to live with her children's choices.*

We all spend time and energy worrying about things we can't change. Sure, Jo's life would be easier if her daughter had waited until she was married to have a child. Things would be much simpler if she had married an African-American man. But she didn't. Besides, those were not Jo's decisions to make. Her daughter has made her choices, and now it is up to Jo to find a way to live with them. Wishing that past events had never occurred is futile. We can't turn back the clock and undo the choices our children have made. Our role in the lives of our grandchildren may depend on how well we learn to live with those choices. If our children have to listen to us complain about their decisions every time they see us, they will probably not want to see us very often.

We may hold ourselves responsible for the choices our grown children have made. When they choose well, we applaud our parenting and their good judgment. When we feel they have chosen poorly, we question our parenting and our children's good sense. These reactions are destructive. Grown children must make their own decisions and take responsibility for them. We are responsible only to learn to live with their choices, getting on with the business of loving our child, his or her mate, and the grandchildren.

Jack was probably not the person Leslie's parents would have picked for her to marry. Some of his values and beliefs conflicted with theirs. Once Leslie made up her mind to marry Jack, however, her parents were solidly behind her and never expressed any dissatisfaction with her choice. Leslie's parents knew that it was not their decision to make, and they did an excellent job of making Jack feel welcome in their family. Now they are grandparents, and their skillful handling of Jack and Leslie's marriage and their understanding of the principle that they had to learn to live with their daughter's choices have put them in a great position as grandparents. If they had protested loudly and often to Leslie about Jack, his resentment and bitterness would have precluded their involvement in the lives of the grandkids.

2. Do not punish your grandchildren for your children's choices. The second principle for grandparenting with a difference is also vitally important. Understand and follow this concept, and grandparenting with a difference will be much easier. *We must not punish our grandchildren for our children's choices*.

One grandfather has never seen his nine-year-old grandson, even though they live only ten miles apart. His daughter married a man of Asian descent. His negative feelings about Asians date from the Korean War, and he has never dealt with them. When his daughter announced her engagement, he threw her out of the house and hasn't spoken to her since. His anger at his daughter's choice is punishing his only grandchild, and punishing himself too. Prejudice has destroyed his opportunity to enjoy his grandson.

We may be angry or disappointed by a decision our son or daughter makes. But we must never turn that anger on our grandchildren. They have done nothing wrong. I am often disappointed by the lack of forgiveness and understanding exercised by Christians. The grandparent mentioned above is an elder in the church, yet I believe he is out of God's favor. He is not only sinning with his prejudice, but also with his anger. He is sinning, too, in his lack of love toward his daughter, her husband, and especially his grandson.

> If anyone says, "I love God," yet hates his brother, he is a liar. For anyone who does not love his brother, whom he has seen, cannot love God, whom he has not seen. And He has given us this command: Whoever loves God must also love his brother. (1 John 4:20–21)

The Bible is clear in its call for love. Although John is talking here about loving our brothers in Christ, we can assume that we should also love our own family members. Disappointment and anger erect huge barriers that we will not or cannot hurdle. You may find yourself reading this book as a surprised and bewildered grandparent. Your unmarried daughter has just given you a grandchild, and you are filled with conflicting feelings of love and anger and joy and disappointment and shame. Don't take those feelings out on your new grandchild. More than anything in the world, your job is to love that little boy or girl. If he's partly of a different race, so be it. If his father is Catholic, Baptist, Jewish, or Buddhist, love him. Don't punish him for choices that his parents have made.

You don't have to turn it into a tragedy when your daughter or son marries somebody from outside your religious background or chooses a mate with an ethnic difference. You don't need to go into high drama when your unmarried son or daughter announces impending parenthood. A greater tragedy occurs when you react with such rage and bitterness that you can never grow close to your grandkids. Biracial babies giggle and laugh just like red and yellow and black and white babies. They all need hugs and love. New parents of every kind need to know that their parents are behind them with love and acceptance and support.

3. Accept your grandchildren the way they are. Remember Reggie's grandparents? Reggie is a special-needs grandchild. His developmental disability has left his grandfather and grandmother concerned about the role they play in his life. As they watch other grandparents at the zoo talk and laugh with their grandchildren, they know that they will probably never have those opportunities with Reggie. He is wheelchair-bound and unable to communicate verbally. Even so, Reggie's grandparents haven't given up. They have learned the third principle of grandparenting with a difference. *Accept your grandchildren the way they are.*

It is futile for Reggie's grandparents to wish that his body would cooperate with his mind. Unless there's a miracle, it's just not going to happen. Instead of stewing in their sorrow, Reggie's grandparents have chosen to accept him as he is and love him without reservation. They do everything with Reggie they would do with a "normal" grandchild. They take him to the zoo, to McDonald's, and to the park. In fact, they do more than most grandparents. Realizing his special needs, they help his parents with his therapy and accompany him on his frequent trips to the hospital. Sometimes it's hard for them to see him in his wheelchair. They know the loving little boy trapped inside that damaged body, and they wish for his sake that he could run and jump like other little boys. But they have learned that, if Reggie's health is a special heartache, his soul is a special joy. They cannot imagine now what life would be like without him.

He has taught them to view life differently. They see every day with Reggie as a gift to be treasured, and they are determined to savor their limited time with him. They are involved, creative grandparents, and they love their special-needs grandson very much.

The principle of accepting your grandchildren as they are holds true no matter what the special need. If your grandchildren don't go to your church, accept them anyway. If they are not growing up with your values, accept them anyway. If they can't hear or see or walk, love and accept them anyway. This can be difficult. It's one thing to say, and another, much more difficult, thing to do.

The keys to accepting special needs grandchildren are honesty and knowledge. Honesty—constant, relentless honesty with ourselves—about how we really feel is vital. We must be honest about our underlying motives, and about our own prejudices. We must also be honest about the reality of the need and the prognosis for recovery. Above all, we must be honest with God.

Acceptance is also made easier by knowledge. If you are the grandparent of a special-needs grandchild, take the time and effort to understand those needs. Find out about his actual abilities, potential, and limitations. Disabled children are often capable of far more than we give them credit for. One mother of a special-needs child had to tell her parents repeatedly to stop babying their granddaughter. Although she is sixteen years old, the grandparents, because of her disability, talked to her as if she were five years old. This was degrading for her, and it angered her mother. Observe the child's developmental age, and learn about both the child's limitations and possibilities. Work with the limitations and strive for the possibilities.

When grandparenting a child from another ethnic

background, take the time to learn as much as you can about that background. This will enable you to understand your grandchildren better and to accept him more easily. The same principle holds true when grandparenting children who are being raised in a different religious atmosphere. Again, learn as much as you can. It will provide you with an opportunity to talk to your grandchildren about their religious values. You may find that the differences are not as great as you had feared. One of the easiest ways to build acceptance is to know your grandchildren.

4. Work for compromise. If religious faith is important to us and not to our children, how can we deal with that difference and still help our grandchildren in their development of faith? A related question is this: How do we pass on our moral values to our grandchildren when our children do not share those values? The answer to both of those questions is found in the fourth principle for grandparenting with a difference: *Be willing to compromise.*

The words *compromise, faith,* and *values* don't usually go together. And we are not suggesting for one minute that grandparents compromise on issues of faith or morality. But let's be realistic. Some opportunity to pass on our faith and moral values is better than none. To have even some chance, we are going to have to stop thinking in terms of winner-take-all. We have to think in terms of what is the best we can do for our grandchildren.

Issues of faith and morality often present themselves in sharp contrasts. Either you are a Christian or you aren't. Either you believe premarital sex is wrong or you don't. These issues are clearly marked. We feel that if we don't chide our children for not attending church or for their lax morals we are implicitly giving their actions our stamp of approval. But wait a minute. This book is not advocating that we abandon our goals of strong moral values for our grandchildren. Nor is it sliding into moral relativism. We believe strongly that some values are *not* open to compromise. The issues are black and white; however, the means of achieving these values in our grandchildren are not so clear.

Let me give an example. Maryanne is a devout Christian. Her daughter hasn't been to church in years. Maryanne feels strongly that her grandchildren should be in church at least once a week. Her daughter doesn't care, and she usually sleeps in on Sunday. Maryanne has asked her daughter if she could take her grandchildren to church with her. Because her daughter doesn't like getting up and getting them dressed for church she said no.

At this point Maryanne had a choice. She could become angry, storm out of the house, and go to church for the rest of her life without her grandchildren. But Maryanne knew the value of compromise. She rightly figured that some church is better than no church at all. So she suggested to her daughter that twice a month her grandchildren could stay with her on Saturday night, and she would take them to church with her on Sunday. Her daughter agreed! Maryanne loves being with her grandchildren every other weekend. She did not compromise her goal of developing her grandchildren's faith, but by compromising on *how* she would reach that goal, she was able to accomplish it.

Another key to compromise is to avoid being judgmental. If we pick up our grandchildren for church and never fail to chastise their parents for not going, we probably won't get the opportunity very often. When we are with our grandchildren and talk about faith or morality, we must avoid criticizing their parent's religious behavior. If we don't, Mom and Dad will understandably see this as an effort to undermine and judge them. Our children will already be defensive about turning away from their faith or from the family's values. They may see judgmentalism and legalism in our every comment or heavy sigh. We can't do anything about that, but we can let them know that even though we don't approve of the direction they are going, we still love them and welcome them into our home.

If we are to have any say in our grandchildren's moral and spiritual development, compromise is necessary. A hard-line attitude may end any opportunity to be a positive religious influence on our grandchildren.

5. Don't worry about the opinions of others. Some of us let ourselves be guided by the prejudices and hang-ups of our friends, neighbors, and fellow church members. We like to believe that we aren't influenced by their attitudes, but the opinions of others do affect us. We need to acknowledge that fact, and to be on our guard when grandparenting with a difference.

You may feel self-conscious the first time you bring your brain-injured grandson to your church. A person like him may never have attended before. You may notice that you leave a trail of whispers behind you as you proudly lead him out to your car following the service. Creative involved grandparents choose not to care. The choice comes down to this: Do I want my grandchild, regardless of his differences, to grow up knowing that I love him and that he is precious to me? Or am I going to let the narrow and sinful thinking of others—even my closest friends—keep me away from him?

If you are reading this book, you have already made

your choice. You have decided that being an involved, creative grandparent is more important than golf, more important than Scrabble, and certainly more important than worrying about what the neighbors think. We must be careful, though. It is easier than we think to be controlled by the attitudes of others. It is possible that we *are* a little ashamed of the difference in our grandchildren. After all, you and I have our share of prejudice. We have held these beliefs for a very long time, and bigotry doesn't disappear with the birth of a grandchild who is "different." Inside we may still feel some shame.

We must deal with those feelings immediately. We cannot pretend they don't exist. They will come out in subtle ways. Our real attitudes will show over time. The first step toward overcoming any misgivings is to admit your struggle with the difference. Many of us live our whole lives acting as if we don't have any problems or prejudice, when in truth we have both. We will not be able to grandparent effectively until we acknowledge our irrational or sinful attitudes.

The second step is to go to our children, confess our feelings to them, and ask for their forgiveness. They need to know that we are serious about loving them and their child. They need to see that we recognize the problems, and that we are committed to dealing with them.

The final step is to seek God's help in renewing our thinking. We need His help to keep our minds free of bigotry and prejudice and embarrassment. Only God can cleanse us from sinful attitudes we have nourished for many years.

Don't allow the ignorant attitudes of others to keep you from being the best grandparent you can be. Tell them how much you love your grandchild. Do it loudly and often. Let everyone hear and see your pride in your "different" grandchild and your pleasure at being with him. This will silence the whispers and do wonders for your grandchild and his family.

6. Follow the biblical mandate to love. Jesus Himself set the best example possible for those of us who are struggling to grandparent with a difference. Sitting beside a well, He talked intimately with a woman of low moral character and of a different nationality. He didn't condemn her or chastise her; He loved her. His example is our mandate. Love your grandchildren and your children. Although life may fling some surprises at you, don't use them as an excuse to become angry and withdraw from your family. We are to love one another, the Bible says, for love is from God (1 John 4:7). I know it's easier said than done, but you can do it—with God's help.

Ed and Jean sat in my office with stony looks on their faces. They were angry at their eighteen-year-old daughter. She had announced to them the week before that she was pregnant, and that the father was a black man. Ed and Jean have many of the prejudices of white middle-class people of their generation, and they were shocked. The pregnancy was bad enough; in reality, it confirmed their worst fears. But the fact that the baby was going to be biracial upset them even more.

When he heard the news, Ed lost his temper at his daughter. He swore that he would kill the father. Jean ran sobbing into the bedroom, her dreams for her daughter demolished. Now Ed and Jean wanted to know what they should do. Their feeling was that they should have no contact with their daughter except to pressure her to give the baby up for adoption. I listened, and then told them they were wrong. They were disappointed and angry, and they were not thinking clearly. I encouraged them to love their daughter through this difficult time. I advised them to try to understand her and her motives. I counseled them to support their daughter even if she went against their wishes and kept the baby. I asked them to consider opening their hearts to this infant life. They thanked me curtly and left, still angry. I didn't think I would ever see them again.

Eight months later, on a sunny afternoon, I was sitting at my desk counseling another couple when my secretary rang in. "Jerry, a couple out here really want to see you."

"Joy, I'm in the middle of something right now, can't it wait?" I answered.

"No, I think you are going to want to see this."

I excused myself and went to see what the big deal was. I was greeted by the smiling faces of Ed and Jean. No, they weren't just smiling, they were grinning from ear to ear. In their arms they were holding their six-week-old grandson. And they were very proud of him. I looked into the blanket and there he was, brown eyes shining brightly.

"Thanks, Jerry. We were mad at you at first. But once we calmed down, we decided to take your advice. And look at our boy. Isn't he the cutest, most special boy you have ever seen?" Ed and Jean both began to weep, and I cried with them that afternoon. Mine were tears of joy. Seeing them with their beautiful baby, I saw the deep, real love of two grandparents for their different grandson. This was grandparenting with a difference!

Dealing with differences? Don't give up. You *can* overcome the obstacles of different ethnic backgrounds or religious beliefs or lifestyles. You *can* creatively grandparent a special-needs child. You *can* grandparent with a difference. If you will remember the six principles:

1. Learn to live with your children's choices.
2. Do not punish your grandchildren for your children's choices.
3. Accept your grandchildren the way they are.
4. Work for compromise.
5. Don't worry about the opinions of others.
6. Follow the biblical mandate to love.

Checklist for grandparenting with a difference

❑ I am willing to accept my child's choice of a life mate?
❑ Social status honestly is not a factor as I think about my child's mate.
❑ I do not feel that my heritage or children are better than others.
❑ I do not make disparaging remarks to my grandchildren about their mom or dad.
❑ I do not carry as much prejudice as I did ten or twenty years ago.
❑ I am no longer angry at God because my grandchild is different.
❑ I have taken concrete steps to bridge the gap between me and my children.
❑ I have researched and read to learn everything I can about my chronically ill or disabled grandchild.
❑ I no longer let the prejudices or opinions of others influence my feelings.
❑ I have talked openly with my child about the differences in our family and that of his or her spouse.
❑ I am able to both love and like those who are different.

Chapter Nine

Faith of Our Fathers

Uncle Herm died a few months ago. He had been battling cancer the last few years of his life, and at age 72, he lost. By most standards, Uncle Herm's life was not noteworthy. He farmed the land his father before him had farmed. He raised his children, went to church, loved his wife. Herm's life hadn't been extraordinary, but his funeral, well, his funeral was special.

The memorial service was traditional, focused on the Bible, and full of hope. A believer in Jesus Christ, Uncle Herm was ready to be translated from this life to the next. His funeral ended with members of his family sharing their memories of him. His five grown grandchildren each took a turn to speak of their grandfather. They said that while they helped him on the farm, he had patiently taught them the arcane skill of coaxing food from the land. They reminisced about harvesting their return from the soil and their grandfather's pride in the job well done.

Uncle Herm's youngest granddaughter stood last. As she began to speak, her voice broke and tears rolled down her cheeks. "My grandfather taught me many things," she said, "and I loved being with him on the farm. But I will always be grateful for what he told me about Jesus. His faith was real and powerful." She held her hand over her chest and said, "I will take his faith with me forever in my heart." I was deeply moved as I listened.

That young lady carries with her the faith of her father and the faith of her father's fathers. As believing grandparents, our most important task is to communicate our faith in Christ to our grandchildren. Uncle Herm knew that. Even though, by most reckonings, he was a man of modest means, he died with riches because his grandchildren loved Jesus.

Communicating our faith to our grandchildren can be a daunting task. Grandchildren want to have fun with Grandpa and Grandma; they don't want to be lectured about God. Grandparents want to make their grandchildren laugh; they don't want to raise the somber issues of Christianity.

Recent research on the role of grandparents has shown that most of us *do not* share our personal faith with our grandchildren, and that we don't have much influence on their beliefs. Many of us have evidently decided that it is *not* our responsibility to share Jesus with our grandchildren. We assume it to be the job of the parents. The primary responsibility for the spiritual education of our grandchildren does fall on their parents. But that doesn't mean we may neglect our responsibility to do our part. Many grandparents simply never try to talk to their grandchildren about faith. We may believe that it is important, and we may pray that our precious grandchildren receive Christ, but it just "never comes up." During visits, most of us have difficulty talking about our faith. This holds true whether talking to our friends on the golf course or our grandchildren in the car. It's not easy or natural for us to bring our relationship with Jesus into the conversation.

We must realize that our grandchildren are growing up in a "post-Christian" society. The overriding beliefs of today are diametrically opposed to the values of Christianity. Our grandchildren are not going to inherit our faith automatically. Every Christian in a child's life must therefore be committed to passing on his faith to that child. The future of our grandchildren demands that their fathers, mothers, uncles, aunts, and especially their grandparents, live out their faith in front of the children. If we don't, we run the risk of losing the second generation to the "spirit of the age." We will lose our grandchildren to the culture; to our decadent, godless society. They will not be influenced by Jesus, but by the world. It has happened before.

Joshua was a mighty man of God. As we read of his exploits in the Bible, we marvel at his faith. We proudly quote his famous phrase; "But as for me and my house, we will serve the Lord" (Josh. 24:15). But we stop there. We need to read a little farther. If we did, we would find that even though Joshua's children went on to serve God, his grandchildren did not. As a matter of fact, Joshua's grandchildren turned away from God and toward wickedness. Why did this happen? We don't have the complete story, but somewhere along the way, we can be sure that somebody didn't get the message that God is at the center of life. Between the declared "we will serve the Lord" and the maturing of Joshua's grandchildren, there was a gap in belief.

I have seen gaps in my faith many times in my experience as a pastor. Grandma was a saint, a pillar of spiritual strength. Mom was a true believer, dedicated to serving God. But granddaughter has no relationship with Jesus. Creative grandparents can have a vital part in making certain that doesn't happen in their family.

If we will make a concerted, consistent effort to live and share our faith in Christ with our grandchildren, we will have a profound influence on them. The Bible gives us not only the example of Joshua, but also the example of Timothy. "I have been reminded of your sincere faith, which first lived in your grandmother Lois and in your mother Eunice and, I am persuaded now lives in you also" (2 Tim. 1:5). Paul credited Timothy's grandmother for beginning the tradition of faith, then handing it down not only to her child, but also to her grandchild. We can impact our grandchildren's lives for Jesus! Lois had a plan to communicate her faith not only with her children but with her grandchildren. In fact, it appears from Scripture that Lois was still influencing Timothy's life while he was moving into a position of prominence in the early church.

As grandparents, we have unfinished business. We want to see our grandchildren take positive steps toward a godly life. Most of us, however, don't stop to think about what it will take to see this unfinished business through. We need a plan to accomplish this most important job. We will not do a good job of communicating our faith to our grandchildren if we do not have a plan.

In this chapter we will suggest a plan for passing the faith of our fathers on to our grandchildren. Taking you through the stages of your grandchildren's development, we will suggest ways to communicate Jesus effectively to them. Ultimately the decision to follow God or turn away from Him is not ours to make. That decision rests squarely on their young shoulders. We cannot make that choice for them. However, in cooperation with their parents, we can live and breathe true Christianity before them every day of their lives. And we can impact their spiritual decisions.

The Wonder Years

Jessica came home from Sunday school and asked her father this question: "Daddy, how can God see me if I can't see Him?" Dad looked to the ceiling for help. He turned his brain inside out trying to figure out how to tell a five-year-old that God is a spirit. "Well, Jessica, God doesn't have a body like you and me. He doesn't have hair. . . ." "But Dad, Jesus did, and He's God—right?" Dad was not thrilled that Jessica had decided to introduce the mystery of the Trinity into this difficult discussion. "Sweetheart, it's hard to explain exactly, but God and Jesus are the same person and yet they are distinct. . . ."

This real-life discussion illustrates the difficulty we may encounter as grandparents who are committed to spiritual education. Wonder-years children will always ask more questions than you and I can answer. And they will continue to ask questions long after we are willing to answer. But that doesn't mean the task is hopeless. The boundless curiosity of young children opens the door for us to teach them about Jesus. Fortunately for us, wonder-years children don't need answers to the profound mysteries of the universe. So we don't need an advanced degree in theology to pass our faith on to them.

Young children need to learn three things about God. First, they need to know that God is with them and that He cares about them. Second, they need to know that God is a person; that He is someone they can talk to at any time and rely on in times of trouble. Third, they need to know that God is in charge; that He is the Creator and Sustainer of the universe. Wonder-years children don't need to understand the Trinity, the book of Revelation, or the latest thinking about the hypostatic union. It is enough for them to know these three fundamental truths.

Children in the wonder years of early childhood are sometimes fearful. One grandmother told of the nightmares her four-year-old granddaughter was experiencing. The child was dreaming regularly about monsters taking away her mom and dad. When she visited Grandma, these dreams became frequent and vivid. Grandma comforted her grandchild with stories from the Bible. She has a gift for storytelling, and she eased the fear in her granddaughter's heart with stirring tales of God's protection. She told how He kept Daniel safe in the den of lions, and how He protected David in the presence of giants. As the child lay down to sleep, Grandma would pray with her, "Dear God, we know You love Nikki. We know that You want the best for her. Please help her sleep without bad dreams. And God, help her to know that You will always be with her, especially when she is afraid, and that You will never, ever leave her."

This grandmother understood that the truth of God's presence brings security to young children who are afraid. She also knew that talking about God's omnipotence or omnipresence wasn't going to accomplish anything. So she did what came naturally, she told stories. Cuddled up in Grandma's arms, her young granddaughter was learning what it means to be safe and secure in Jesus.

Through her simple prayers, this grandmother also communicated the second important truth wonder-years children need to know about God: He is a person and a friend in time of need. Abstract concepts of God mean little to young children. Their minds are not capable of grasping the idea of an all-powerful, all-knowing Being. They need God brought down to life. They need a God they can talk to and One who listens to them. They need the God of the Bible.

Praying before meals is not always the highest expression of spirituality. But in our house, we never eat without thanking God for the food and for all His gifts to us. We feel this helps our grandchildren. We believe strongly that if they are to see God as One who cares about them, they must see us talk with God. So we pray before every meal. We feel it is an excellent way for us to teach them that God listens to us and hears us.

Wonder-years grandchildren are very much at the mercy of arbitrary forces they do not understand. If Mom and Dad separate, a two- or three-year-old child is left wondering when Daddy is coming home. If the family moves, the child has no idea what has become of her playmates, her old room, and her favorite spot in the yard. For this reason, as well as for reasons of safety and security, our wonder-years grandchildren need to know that God is in charge of the world. They need to see God as the One who made the stars and the sun. They need to be reassured that even though things sometimes get scary, and things happen to us that we don't understand, the God who made the trees and the flowers, the God who fashioned us with His own hands, is in control.

Tom, a creative grandfather, often takes his three grandchildren to the park. They walk among the tall trees, lush grass, beautiful flowers, and green bushes. Tom is an amateur botanist, and he points out the names and characteristics of the flora and fauna they see on their walks. Tom consistently reminds his grandchildren that God made all the beautiful things they are seeing. He tells them that God created everything that is in the world, even the stars that twinkle at them when they go to bed. Then Grandpa Tom stops walking, crouches down to eye level with his young grandchildren and says, "The same

God who made all of this made you and loves you. He is watching over you right now. God knows you inside and out and He loves who you are." Then Tom straightens up and continues his walk. Tom knows what his wonder-years grandchildren need to know about God. He doesn't waste their time with sermons or preaching. Instead, he creatively finds ways to express the love and concern God has for them. This in time eases their fears.

Our wonder-years grandchildren may never grow up to be great theologians. But we will have accomplished a great deal if they go through the early years of their life feeling safe in the arms of a loving God. Three-year-olds don't know anything about propitiation or eschatology, but they know fear and they know what it feels like to be held and loved. If we can communicate to them that God holds them in His powerful arms and loves them all the time, we will have done much to guide them toward the path of following Jesus.

The Middle Years

"Grandpa, I need to ask you a question. But it's kind of stupid."

"Well, John, why don't you just go ahead and ask me? Let me decide if it's stupid or not."

"I feel kind of dumb, but you are the only one I can talk to about this. Promise me that you won't tell Mom. She would really be mad."

"I'll tell you what, John. You tell me what's bothering you, and I promise to keep it between you and me if I feel that you aren't going to hurt yourself or another person."

"Oh, Grandpa, it's nothing like that. It's just that, well I was wondering if God still loves us even when we do something bad."

"John, I'm sixty-two years old. I do something or say something that I shouldn't every single day. But from the day I became a Christian, almost forty-five years ago, I have known that God loves me—even when I mess up, even when I do something bad. He loves you too, John. You are nine right now. Every day for the rest of your life you are going to have to make decisions about the right thing to do. Sometimes you will make the wrong choice. But know this, my boy, God will never stop loving you because of what you do, never, ever. And, listen close: neither will I. By the way, what happened that made you ask this question?"

We can be a terrific help to our middle years grandchildren (ages six to eleven) in their search for a growing up faith. Kids in these years between the cuteness of the wonder years and the turmoil and emotional growth of adolescence are making life-changing decisions about their faith. They need their creative, involved grandparents to help light the way.

The one key to helping our grandchildren is this: School-age children need a hero of their faith. And that is where you and I come in. Creative, involved grandparents can be heroes of the faith to children desperately searching for someone to look up to and believe in. At this stage of development, boys need to identify with men and girls need to identify with women. Boys and girls need to see us as men and women who live out our Christianity heroically.

Now, don't misunderstand. I'm not suggesting that we sell all of our earthly possessions and move to the Galapagos Islands as pioneer missionaries. That is not what I mean by *heroic*. To middle-years children, heroes are simply people who keep the promises they make. Heroes of the faith are Christians who live up to what they claim to be. Elementary age children living in the last decade of the twentieth century are remarkably cynical. Many of them have been lied to by their parents—and they know it. They have seen Mom or Dad leave and never return. They have lived with the broken promises of workaholic parents, who keep promising to take them to Disney World but who never seem to find the time. At an early age they learn the language of excuse and rationalization. "I'm sorry I didn't make it to see you in the school play, Nate. I know I promised I would, but I had to work late." "Holly, you know that you are very important to me, but mommy has to go away. I'll visit you at Christmas, and we'll see you during summer vacation. Good-bye." The hearts of children like these are littered with the refuse of broken promises. If they haven't experienced it personally, they have observed it first-hand in the lives of their friends and classmates. These kids need a hero, someone they can trust no matter what. Grandparents can be that role model of faith.

Creative grandparents who want to become faith-heroes to their middle-years grandchildren need to build three character qualities into their lives: integrity, endurance, and courage. By modeling these three character qualities, we can encourage our middle years grandchildren to follow Jesus for the rest of their lives.

A hero has integrity. American culture in these last years of the twentieth century has precious little integrity. Children are starving for truth. They need someone they can trust implicitly and always. Their inability to find adults who live with integrity has a devastating affect on their development of faith. Every year Jack spends part of his summers taking junior-high and senior-high school students on mission trips to the inner city. During one of his visits, he got to know a ten-year-old boy who was growing up in one of the poorest sections of the country. Jack was trying to tell him that Jesus loved him and wanted to have a relationship with him. This little boy, Thomas, just kept shaking his head. Exasperated at his inability to get through to Thomas, Jack almost shouted, "What's wrong? Why do you just keep shaking your head?"

Thomas looked up and said, "My daddy told me that he loved me, but he's gone, and Mamma said that he ain't ever gonna come back. Then my mamma, she started drinking, and I don't see her much anymore." The little guy's voice trailed off. Jack was at a loss for words. Then Thomas' face brightened and he said, "But my grandma takes care of me now, and she always does what she says. She told me that she was going to whup my behind if I didn't come straight home from this meeting yesterday, and I believed her. She's always tough on me and my sisters, but she loves us."

Further conversation revealed that Thomas' grandmother is a serious Christian, and that her influence on ten-year-old Thomas is profound. Nobody else who is important in his life followed through on their commitments. Every single person let him down except his tough-love grandmother.

You and I need to build integrity into our lives. We need to follow through on our commitments to our grandchildren. If we say we are going to do something for or with them, then we had better do it! If we say that we are Christians and want our grandchildren to follow Jesus, then we had better live as followers of Jesus. Our grandchildren do not need another person in their lives who

speaks one way and acts another. If we want our grandchildren to see us as heroes of the faith, then we need to
live with integrity. We cannot fool our school-age grandchildren for long. They are very good at seeing through our
facades and our pretensions. They will find us out.

When they see our integrity, school-age children receive a sense of security. They know that in a world of
broken promises, Grandma's word is always to be trusted. There is a warmth there, a security blanket of trust.
That trust is then transferred to God. If no one who really counts to a child keeps his promises, it will be very difficult for him to believe that God does. Whether we like
it or not, school-age children's ideas of God are profoundly influenced by their relationships with adults. In other
words, when our grandchildren see us, in effect they are
seeing God. If we tell them about our faith and then let
them down by breaking our promises, they may extend
that disappointment to their feelings about God. This is
a difficult burden to shoulder, I know. But those are the
facts. Therefore, we need to be people of integrity, heroes
of faith to our middle-years grandchildren.

A hero perseveres. Our grandchildren need to see us endure,
even when things get difficult. When life doesn't turn
out the way we would choose, when our children get divorced or our families suffer tragedy, our middle-years
grandchildren need to see someone's faith hold strong.
They need to see that God is there for us when times are
tough, strengthening and upholding us.

One grandmother illustrated endurance to her
grandson by talking honestly about her fight against cancer. As he saw her body slowly waste away, this boy saw
his grandmother fight and fight. She never quit trying to

live. She never stopped believing that God was in control. And through the entire painful ordeal, she would tell him through her pain and his tears, "Hush, child. God is here, you know. He won't let me down. Even if I die, I know He won't let me down. Listen to your Grandma. If we only followed Jesus when it was easy, well, that wouldn't take much faith, would it? Faith in God is proven by keeping it when things get tough. Believe me, things are tough right now. . . ."

Endurance is the ability to keep going when everyone around us is telling us to quit. When everything inside cries out, "Enough!" By living life with perseverance, we show our impressionable school-age grandchildren that God is by our side day and night, through good and bad. We show them that Christianity is far more than just going to church or saying grace before the evening meal. Our grandchildren see that our faith in God is what keeps us going when life is hard and unfair.

We live in an age of ease. Many in our society do not keep going when things get tough. We whine. We drink. We do drugs. We separate and divorce. We leave jobs. Our grandchildren are growing up ready to quit when things don't go their way. A Christianity characterized by endurance is the best antidote for that poison. Unless they see perseverance modeled, our grandchildren may be tempted to fall away from God when temptation strikes. They may feel that if they mess up too much, God may give up on them. Our endurance shows them that God never gives up on them, and that He is a friend who will never leave them.

A hero has courage. Our grandchildren are watching us. They need grandparents who exhibit courage. It takes courage to follow Jesus. It takes courage to leave a job that requires us to act unethically, or to stay with one that is unfair and demanding. Your grandchildren will see that kind of courage as heroic. It takes courage to stay with a difficult marriage. Your school-age grandchildren will know it. It takes courage to admit that you've done something foolish. Your grandchildren will see it. It takes courage to tell your grandchildren about Jesus, to let them know how important He is to your everyday life.

Along with providing a good example, telling stories of faith is a great way to teach courage. Stories about other children who chose to do the right thing when it was very hard. Stories of people who have been extraordinarily courageous in their love for others and God. Tell them stories about adults who took the hard way instead of the easy way out. Tell them the great old missionary stories of William Carey, Adoniram Judson, Hudson Taylor, and Jim Elliot. Tell them about the biblical heroes of the faith—and not just the stories they've known since they were toddlers. Let them see that courage is an integral part of the Christian life. Then challenge them to live courageously by making courageous choices every day.

Middle-years children need a hero to show them Jesus. Not Superman or Batman, not even super-Christian. Just a grandma who keeps her promise. Just a grandpa who keeps going when it's tough. Just a grandma and grandpa who do the right thing when it's easier to do wrong.

One good way to illustrate integrity, endurance, and courage is to create a family history of faith. Middle-years children get a sense of what has gone before, the sacrifices made by others in their family, when grandparents take the time to retell the family story of faith. Tell it with verve and excitement. Let your grandchildren see that they were not the first to feel fear at following Jesus. Show them the heroic faith of others in the family. That faith history may have started with you. It may have been going on for 200 years, which gives them a sense that they are a part of something far bigger than themselves. Inspire your grandchildren to carry on as heroes of the faith by living with integrity, endurance, and courage.

Just a word of warning. By providing our grandchildren with a hero of the faith, I am not suggesting that you fake a perfect life. Nor am I trying to make you feel guilty for being human. Instead, I am encouraging a real-life faith lived out in full view of your school-age grandchildren. We can do it, you and I. We can become heroes of the faith to our grandchildren. We can show our questioning seven-year-old granddaughter that Christianity works, and that we wouldn't live without Jesus for one minute. We can make a profound impact on their lives, not by playing Superman, but by living our lives with integrity, endurance, and courage.

The Teen Years
"Grandpa, I don't know what I believe anymore. I've been going to church forever and listening to Mom and Dad talk about God all my life, but I don't know what I think is true. Sometimes this stuff about God and Jesus makes a lot of sense; other times it just feels like a bunch of religious garbage. I'm going to be a senior next year, and Dad says that he wants me to be baptized. I don't think I want to be baptized because I'm not sure what I believe about God anymore. What should I do? How can I explain this to Dad? He's going to flip his lid."

Some of your teenage grandchildren may struggle tremendously with their faith. They may doubt, cast off their belief, and live rebellious lives. Others, however, may become leaders in their youth group, attend Bible studies, and talk openly with their friends at school about Jesus. Most likely though, they will be somewhere in the middle. Their Christian lives will be characterized by apathy and a lack of growth. What's a grandparent to do? We want our grandchildren to be Christian leaders and devoted followers of Jesus. The idea of them becoming bored with Christianity or, even worse, turning away from their heritage of faith sickens us with worry. The question we ask is, "Can we do anything to help?"

The answer is yes. You and I, as creative grandparents, can do some very good things. But we cannot guarantee anything. We must remember that teenagers are nearly adults, and that they are responsible for their own decisions. We cannot make them believe, nor can we force them to follow Jesus. But we can play a major role in their development of faith.

Adolescents need a road map of reality. During the years of adolescence our grandchildren begin to stake out their belief systems. They start to separate what they really, truly believe from what they have just been told all their lives. They need help and guidance in figuring these things out. They need a road map to help them negotiate the twists and turns of the road to adulthood.

But many adolescents aren't getting that help, that road map of reality, from their grandparents. Quentin Schultz was one of the writers of an insightful book on media and popular culture titled *Dancing in the Dark*. He stated that the media—especially music, television, and movies—have become the average teenager's road map of reality. Media and popular culture largely define our grandchildren's tastes and attitudes. Their sounds and visual images help teenagers determine what is right and wrong, acceptable and unacceptable. Just two things occupy more time in a teenager's life than television and music: sleeping and school.

This presents a problem for creative grandparents. We want our grandchildren to follow Jesus, but they can't hear Him over the noise of their lives. Days filled with the pressures of performing in school, the distractions of music and movies, and the entertainment of television leave precious little space for anything else. We want to be part of their lives, but when we look at the world of the American teenager we feel antiquated and intimidated. Our teenage grandchildren's lives are moving so fast that when we do try to enter them, we feel caught in a whirlwind of activity. "Hey Grandpa, how are you doing? I'd love to talk with you, but I've got to be at work by 3:00. After that is track practice and then I'm going over to Theresa's house. Do you mind telling Mom and Dad that I won't be home until late? Thanks. See ya." It will be difficult, but we have to find a way to slow our teenage grandchildren down so we can learn to love them and their crazy ways. We need to help them put on the brakes, to have time to think. Our role in the spiritual development of our grandchild is to help them hear the call of God over the noise in their lives. It is up to us to "pump up the volume," to quote a popular movie, and help our teenage grandchildren become followers of Jesus.

Slowing these teenagers down is not easy. They have attention spans roughly the length of a rock music video. They are part of a generation that has to have everything now. Waiting is not in their lifestyle. Yet this very impatience with life fuels within teenagers a sense of loss. They know that they are missing out on something, but can't seem to jump off the treadmill. Grandparents can help.

If slowing down your adolescent grandchildren so they can hear God's call in their lives is important to you, then you must be prepared to spend time with them. Only when they are in your presence, without the interference of media and peers and school, will they listen to you. So take the time to be with them. If you travel, invite your adolescent grandchild with you on your trips. One grandparent asked her fifteen-year-old grandson to accompany her on a trip to California. He enthusiastically agreed. He asked when they were flying out and was surprised to learn that they would be driving from Michigan to California. Her grandson spent three weeks in her company, much of it confined in a car. Not a bad way to slow down a teenage grandchild so that he can listen to God! This grandmother took the opportunity to talk to her grandson, to find out what was happening in his life, and to interact with him. And he shared with her his struggles with self-confidence, his attempt to make sense of the world, and his worries about the future.

You might want to consider inviting your grandchildren to your house for a few days. Or volunteer to house-sit for their parents if they are leaving on a vacation without one of their teenagers. Creative grandparents find a way to be one-on-one with their grandchildren, to build a relationship and to slow them down.

Slowing them down is the first step. Once we get their world quiet enough for them to hear God, we must teach them to listen to Him. Many things keep them from hearing God. So we must help by removing the obstacles. Teenagers these days routinely bring up three or four major objections to following Jesus. These students are concerned about the hypocritical lives they see many Christians living. They are concerned with injustice, and they ponder the reasons God could let the world become so cruel. They wonder how God could care about them when they feel so small and insignificant. They have low self-esteem, and they haven't always felt love and acceptance from their parents. Grandparents can help teenagers work through these obstacles.

To accomplish this task, we need to be honest, tolerant, and available. As we faithfully become these things to our adolescent grandchildren, we will have a growing impact on their spiritual development.

Be honest. To remove the obstacles between teenagers and God, grandparents must first be honest. High school and junior high students are sick and tired of being lied to. They have been sold a bill of goods by American popular culture, and many of them are starting to realize it. Parents have never been completely truthful with many of them. And when it comes to Christianity, they have been told some of the biggest lies of all. They have been led to believe that becoming a follower of Jesus will make their lives easier. They've been told that Christians don't have the same problems as non-Christians. Teenagers have heard it preached that God will solve all of their problems. But they have seen that it doesn't always work out that way. After accepting Jesus, they still struggle with self-esteem, lust, anger, and the very same problems they worried about before. Teens have seen the public moral failures of well-known Christian figures. As a result, they have become cynical, feeling that nobody is telling them the truth.

If you and I are relentlessly, completely honest with our teenage grandchildren, we can help them see that not all Christians are hypocrites. If we tell them the truth about life—that it is hard and difficult even for Christians—we will build a credibility that is not easily lost. If we share with them our doubts and struggles, letting them see our humanity, we will help them become less judgmental of failure in others. The best way to overcome the obstacle of hypocrisy is to admit to our adolescent grandchildren that we are all hypocrites. Confess that no one can live up to the high standards of Jesus. Then, tell them clearly that He loves us, and that He forgives our failures. A grandparent who converses with his grandchild openly and honestly about faith will gradually tear down the wall that the teen has built up between himself and God. Do it! Be honest with your adolescent grandchildren. Teens are tired of looking up to someone, only to be disappointed. The only way you can overcome that problem is to tell them the truth about life from the start.

Victor was a troubled seventeen-year-old who was sent to live with his grandparents on a farm more than 200 miles away from his suburban home. He had been in a few scrapes with the law and his mother was at her wits' end. Victor's grandfather and grandmother, Henry and Dorothy, volunteered to have him in their home for the summer. The first day there, Victor was angry and sullen. He was obviously uncomfortable with the situation and upset at having been sent away. Henry asked him to do some chores and left him alone. When he returned, Victor was sitting on the fence, his chores undone. "What happened, Victor? I asked you to weed the garden and you haven't even got your fingers dirty."

"I'm not going to weed a stupid garden. I never wanted to live here anyway. You can't make me do anything!"

Grandpa paused almost a full minute before answering. During the growing discomfort of the silence, Victor stared determinedly at the ground. "Victor, you are absolutely right. I cannot physically make you do anything. You look pretty strong, and you are a whole lot younger than I am. I bet if we wrestled, you would beat me in nothing flat. That is why I *asked you* to weed the garden instead of *telling you*. Now, on this farm everybody works hard and plays hard. But nobody eats until they have worked. Here is your job for the day. Weed this garden. Then we'll go into town tonight. But Victor, if you don't work, you won't eat."

As Grandpa walked slowly away, Victor turned his words over in his mind. He didn't believe that his grandfather wouldn't let him eat. So he didn't weed the garden. Suppertime came, and when Victor went into the house he saw that there wasn't a place set for him. His grandmother, a kind woman with laugh wrinkles lining her face, looked at him gravely. "Victor, the garden isn't weeded. I'm sorry, but you are not welcome at this table." She turned around and walked into the kitchen. Victor couldn't believe his ears. His grandparents were serious. He thought about running away, but where would he go? So he went to bed, stubborn and hungry.

At about 2:00 a.m. he woke up, as hungry as he had ever been in his life. He found a flashlight, went out into the garden, and started to weed. After about a half an hour he heard the screen door on the front porch open and close. A few moments later Grandpa was next to him, pulling out weeds. Victor felt stupid. He didn't say anything for a few minutes. His grandpa finally looked at him and said; "Victor, I'm not the best grandpa in the world. But know this, I'll never lie to you. When I say something I will follow through on it. We've done enough for one night. Why don't you come inside and we'll find some leftovers."

During that summer, Victor talked to his grandfather as he had never talked to anyone else. His grandfather had proven that he was honest, and Victor felt like he could share anything with him. Two weeks before he was supposed to go home, Victor and grandpa finished up one of their low-key, periodic talks about God. Victor silently asked God to take him in as one of His children. That was twenty years ago, and Victor still remembers that summer of discovery. "My grandfather was the only person in my life who never lied to me. When he told me about Jesus, I believed him. I still do."

Be tolerant. If we are to help our grandchildren listen to Jesus, we must be tolerant. Adolescents will say things that will turn our hair gray. They like to make outrageous remarks and watch for our response. Grandparents who fly off the handle or who do not allow for some diversity will never be able to help their grandchildren grow up in their faith. While our teenage grandchildren are testing out their beliefs and trying on values for size, they often make outrageous remarks. They are trying to figure out what they believe. It's easy for us to overreact. We wish that they would just accept our beliefs and follow Jesus without question. But true belief must always be a free choice. We can force our grandchildren to act certain ways, and with our disapproving looks and scowls we can even force them to say the "right thing." But we cannot force belief on them. They must be allowed to search out their own values and come to their own faith. Admittedly, an element of risk is involved in letting teenagers do that. There is always the chance they won't decide to follow Jesus. This is a chance we must take. Our grandchildren must know that we love them and support them as they wrestle with the issues of faith.

Sarah is a twenty-two-year-old college graduate. Her father is a minister. In his house there was no room for diversity. No one could question his beliefs and values. Sarah's father is a good man and he loves her, but he is very rigid. He refuses to allow his very bright daughter any intellectual freedom. After graduation from her Christian high school, Sarah enrolled at a state university and majored in education. By the time she graduated, Sarah was telling everyone that she no longer believed in God and that Christianity is ridiculous. Her parents are blaming the secular-humanist education she received at the state university. Maybe they are right. But it is also possible that forcing Sarah into unquestioning belief, refusing to be tolerant or to allow her to grow up in her faith while she was still a teenager, cost Sarah her belief in God. Instead of reaching out in love to guide Sarah gently as she moved from a childhood acceptance of her parents' faith into a vital adult faith of her own, Sarah's parents stood in judgment of her all through college and watched her turn away from God.

Creative grandparents understand that part of the job of adolescents is to formulate their belief system. Those who want to help mold their teenage grandchildren's faith realize that an inflexible, judgmental spirit will turn them away from God. But if we can tolerate our teenager's off-the-wall thoughts, we will gain credibility and be in a position of influence with that teen. While Jack was in high school, he nearly left Christianity. He said some things that were, quite frankly, heresy. He turned to me once when he was seventeen, while I was worried about whether he would ever be a follower of Jesus, and said: "I'm only seventeen, I'm trying to figure out what I believe. Don't I have the right to try and put it all together? Do I have to have all the answers right now? Or do I get some time to figure them out?"

Jack was right. Grandparents who want to help their grandchildren overcome the obstacles blocking faith and a relationship with Jesus need to be tolerant. Give your grandchild some space to grow up in his or her faith. At sixteen or eighteen, they don't have to have it all figured out. By being tolerant, we can maintain a position of influence and respect as our grandchildren sort their way through their beliefs.

Be available. If we are going to help our adolescent grandchildren come to faith in Jesus, we must also be available. We must be the kind of people our grandchildren feel comfortable approaching about everything. The time will come when our adolescent grandchildren, in the middle of trying to formulate a personal belief system, will need the sage counsel of an older and wiser person. By maintaining an attitude of availability and openness, we may become that privileged person. But we must lay the groundwork in advance. To think that we can walk up to our seventeen-year-old granddaughter who doesn't know us very well or see much of us and say, "Whenever you need to talk, I'm right here!" is ludicrous. For us to be of influence in the faith decisions of our grandchildren, we need to establish a pattern of availability early in their lives. We need not live near our grandchildren to do this. We can let them know that they can call us collect any time of the day or night, for any reason.

One grandmother has a real skill of making herself available to her grandchildren. She has been a fixture in their lives since their childhood. When she retired and moved away, she called them often and encouraged them to call her. When they called, she *listened*. Now her grandchildren are in their twenties and she still speaks to them every week. As a matter of fact, her granddaughter just called for advice about a relationship she is in. She asked Grandma if she thought God cares about who she marries. Now, that is a grandma who is available, and who is still playing an important role in her granddaughter's faith development.

Teenagers have a profound need for someone who will listen to them and take them seriously. It's sometimes difficult for teens to speak with their parents about faith, and yet they are in desperate need of adult guidance. Creative, honest, tolerant, available grandparents are in a perfect position to provide understanding and encouragement during their teenage grandchildren's crises of faith.

Nothing should be more important to Christian grandparents than to see their grandchildren grow up to follow Jesus. Still, many of us turn pale at the thought of participating in their spiritual education. We are afraid to talk to our grandchildren about Jesus. The purpose of this chapter has been to give you the inspiration and information necessary to carry out that all-important task. The road is long, and our grandchildren may take many detours. But we can help them grow up to be devout Christians. We can help them choose to follow Jesus. Our story can be that of Eunice, Lois, and Timothy: faith passed down from generation to generation, each new generation growing stronger in Christ than the one before.

Checklist for creative grandparents

❏ I work hard at keeping my personal faith alive and strong.

❏ I accept the challenge of contributing to the spiritual development of my grandchildren.

❏ I don't insist that they believe and do everything exactly as I do.

❏ I try not to be too shocked when they express beliefs that are different than mine, or admit that they are working things through.

❏ Whenever they want to talk about God, I am ready to listen.

❏ I find ways to be alone with my teenage grandchildren, away from all the noise of our society.

❏ I keep every promise I make to my grandchildren.

❏ I can risk letting them know that living for Christ is sometimes a struggle for me too.

❏ I can talk about my faith in Jesus easily and matter-of-factly with my grandchildren.

❏ I have told my grandchildren about my personal history of faith.

Afterword

Just Do It!

At his college graduation, Ronald wept silently when he looked out into the audience and saw his grandparents. They themselves were fighting to hold back tears of pride and joy. You see, Ronald's grandparents were creative, involved grandparents. After his father left home when Ronald was only seven, they had become his best friends. His mother worked two jobs to keep food on the table. But Grandpa and Grandma were always there. While Ronald was growing up, few people in his life believed that he would amount to anything. Just his mom—and his grandma and grandpa. They always told him that he was smart enough to make it through college, that he was good enough to achieve his dreams. He never really believed them, but they never stopped telling him, "You can do it, Ron!" "Go for it, Ron!" "We believe in you, Ron!" Now at his college graduation with an honors cord draped around his neck, Ronald is weeping with joy. His grandparents are weeping too, and he is telling them, "I couldn't have made it without you."

Sheila looked out the window of the airplane that was carrying her 10,000 miles from home. She thought about the people who had influenced her life the most. Her fondest and deepest memories were of her grandmother, a godly woman who instilled in her grandchildren a strong love for Jesus. As Sheila flew toward her first term as a medical missionary in Irian Jaya, her grand-mother's words echoed through her mind, "Whatever happens, Sheila, I'm proud of you. You are doing the hard thing and remaining faithful to God's call on your life." Her medical school friends thought she was crazy to trade a promising career for an uncertain future in the jungles of Indonesia. But she knew better. She was doing what her grandma had taught her.

Creative grandparents have a profound effect on their grandchildren. We may not realize our influence until they are adults, when we can see the principles they live by and the people they are. Rest assured, though, that whatever the outcome, grandparenting creatively is one of life's most rewarding experiences. This isn't just because of the results we see in our grandchildren, but because of what happens inside of us.

Creative grandparenting changes us. We become different people through our involvement with our grandchildren. We are shaped by our grandparenting experiences, even as we are attempting to shape our grandchildren. We are moved to tears of joy and frustration. We are never the same.

Creative grandparenting changes us in at least three ways. First, we draw closer to God. Our faith becomes more important to us. Second, we become more concerned with the legacy we leave behind for our children and our children's children. Third, we live fuller, more joyful lives.

As you and I pass along our values and see our grandchildren make decisions to follow Jesus, we are reminded of what is truly important in life. We see anew that Jesus must be the center of life, and that everything else is secondary. As a pastor and a grandparent, I have no doubt about which role is more spiritually demanding for me. It is harder for me to consistently live the life of a Christian in front of my grandchildren than to live that life in front of my congregation. I have become painfully aware of where I fall short as a follower of Jesus because I have become increasingly aware of how much my grandchildren are looking to me to lead them on the road of faith. It drives me to prayer. Creative grandparents who make spiritual encouragement a priority will do some serious soul searching. They will be drawn closer to God as they see where they need to work and grow as Christians.

We will also be changed by becoming more concerned with the legacy we leave our families after we are gone. I'm not talking about the estate, our earthly possessions. I'm talking about the intangible things from us that our children and grandchildren will carry with them for the rest of their lives. My hope and prayer is that my grandchildren remember the fun and the good times that we had together. More important, I want them to remember me as a man who loved God with all his heart and all his strength. And I want them to carry the knowledge with them for the rest of their lives that I believed in them, and that I thought they were the greatest in the world. That is the legacy I want to leave my descendants.

As we grow into our roles as creative grandparents, the importance of our legacy grows. It changes the way we act and the decisions we make. Leaving behind a nice home and cash in the bank becomes less important. We want to leave a legacy of love and acceptance that becomes legendary. We want our grandchildren to tell their grandchildren how much Grandpa and Grandma loved them and believed in them.

Finally, creative grandparenting changes us by forcing us to live the last third of our lives to the fullest, every single day. Involved grandparents become energetic and exciting people, willing to try new things and risk the unknown. Our grandchildren may not keep us from physically aging, but they do give us plenty of reason to get up in the morning and to treat each new day as a gift from God. An eighty-nine-year-old man says that, after all these years, it is his relationship with his grandchildren that keeps him going. He loves to spend time with them, and they are frequent guests in his nursing home. Creative grandparents live with a profound sense of joy and purpose. Their lives overflow with love, and they are moved and changed by their encounters with their grandchildren.

Creative grandparenting. It's not just an act, and we can't fake it. It is a way of life, a conscious choice to throw caution to the wind and to dive into the lives of our grandchildren with reckless abandon. My deepest desire is that the stories and suggestions in this book have filled you with the longing to make a difference in the lives of your grandchildren. Take the challenge. Be a creative grandparent.

25 creative things you can do with your grandchildren
A guide to some outrageous, crazy, costly, and inexpensive ways to love your grandchildren.

1. Establish a regular "date" with them once a month.
2. Buy them a snake and keep it at your house.
3. Surprise them by picking them up from school and spending the night in a tent along the lake shore or at a fancy hotel beside the pool.

4. Keep a scrapbook of all their accomplishments and present it to them on their wedding day.

5. Write a family history with them as coauthors and researchers.

6. Take a trip with them and ride the five biggest roller coasters in America.

7. Take your grandchild on a missions trip to the inner city or a third-world country.

8. Let your teenage granddaughter style your hair in a way that she thinks is fashionable.

9. Teach your grandchildren how to drive.

10. Get a personal 800-number so your grandkids can call you toll-free.

11. Send them birthday cards in five different languages.

12. Ask them to teach you a skill or hobby.

13. Spend a day at school with them.

14. Spend one evening a month watching your television shows together.

15. Have T-shirts made with you and your grandchild's face on them, and wear them the next time you go out together.

16. Call your grandchildren every other day and tell them in a different way how special they are to you.

17. Let them design the "dream trip" they have always wanted to take, and then go!

18. On a regular basis, work with your grandchildren at a local food bank or homeless shelter.

19. If you have never finished your degree, when they start college, go back with them.

20. Read the entire Bible together in a year.

21. Buy a Nintendo set and play it until you can beat your grandson. Then hold a family video game tournament.

22. Take them with you when you vote and let them pull the levers.

23. Go shopping and let them pick out your next suit or dress.

24. Take them on a business trip with you.

25. Learn to skydive with your grandkids.

Note to the Reader